ONE HUNDRED HILL WALKS IN THE LAKE DISTRICT

Other books in the same series:

One Hundred Hill Walks Around Glasgow by John Chalmer (third edition)

One Hundred Hill Walks Around Edinburgh by John Chalmers and Derek Storey (second edition)

One Hundred Hill Walks From Liverpool by Jim Grindle

One Hundred Hill Walks Around Birmingham by Richard Shurey

ONE HUNDRED HILL WALKS IN THE LAKE DISTRICT

JIM GRINDLE

Series Editor
JOHN CHALMERS

MAINSTREAM
PUBLISHING

EDINBURGH AND LONDON

First published in Great Britain in 1994 by
MAINSTREAM PUBLISHING COMPANY
(EDINBURGH) LTD
7 Albany Street
Edinburgh EH1 3UG

ISBN 1 85158 609 1

A catalogue record for this book is available from the British Library

Typeset in Times by Litho Link Ltd, Welshpool, Powys, Wales
Printed by Great Britain by The Cromwell Press, Melksham, Wiltshire

CONTENTS

OUTLINE MAP

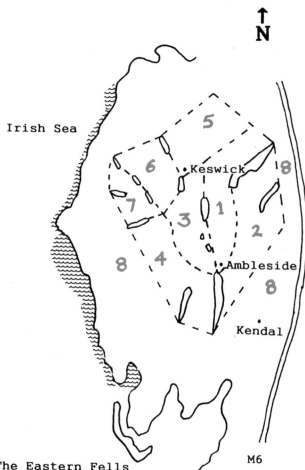

1. The Eastern Fells
2. The Far Eastern Fells
3. The Central Fells
4. The Southern Fells
5. The Northern Fells
6. The North-Western Fells
7. The Western Fells
8 The Outlying Fells

ABOUT THIS BOOK

I have found numbers of people who enjoy walking in the Lake District but who confine themselves to the valleys because they are apprehensive of the felltops and have difficulty in map-reading. This book is a practical guide to help them in planning and when on the hills. It will be of particular use to those who wish to branch out on their own. Any walker who starts out with the shorter and easier routes and gradually progresses to the more difficult will acquire the confidence to plan his or her own days on the hill. If that is not your aim, the book will still help you to enjoy some of the wildest and most beautiful scenery in the British Isles.

To make the book more manageable it has been divided into eight sections. A number of ways of doing this were considered but in the end I decided on the divisions used by Wainwright in his books on the Lakeland fells. This leads to a few anomalies as his last volume was an afterthought and some adjacent walks are in different sections but it does mean that you can refer easily to Wainwright if you wish.

Where walks can be shortened there are notes to tell you how to go about it. In a number of cases walks can be combined to give longer routes, e.g. 16 and 17, 54 and 55 or 81 and 82.

ACKNOWLEDGMENTS

I would like to thank my friends Arthur Pugh and Alan Roberts for their help in the production of this book. Arthur did all the darkroom work on the photographs while Alan not only shared much of the walking in very indifferent weather but also provided invaluable back-up which freed me for the tasks of preparation and recording. June was as supportive as ever.

I would also like to acknowledge the use of the Gordon Walker Chalet at Stair near Keswick which the Lake District Area of the Ramblers' Association made available to me as a member. More than half of the walks in the book were easily reached from it. All walkers in the Lake District must be indebted to the staff of the National Park authority and of the National Trust. Their work in waymarking and the restoration of paths that I have seen deteriorate during my years on the hills have added greatly to the pleasure of researching this book. I can forgive them for leaving a pickaxe near the summit of Dale Head.

The book is dedicated to Margaret and David, two of the best.

NOTES

1. The sketch maps are intended to give a quick visual idea of each walk. They are not to scale and do not replace the Ordnance Survey maps, the appropriate sheet of which should always be used. The 1:50,000 Landranger series or the 1:25,000 Outdoor Leisure series are recommended. The relevant maps for each walk are noted at the beginning of each description. Occasionally a route will require two maps.
2. The 'walking distance' includes an allowance for the continuous variations from the route as it would be measured on the map. It is always necessary on a hill walk to make short detours to avoid bogs, rocks, hillocks, etc. Even with this allowance, the resultant figure must be approximate.
3. The 'amount of climbing' is the sum of all the uphill sections of the route.
4. Distances given within the text are approximations meant for guidance only and are given in metres only.
5. Compass bearings given in the text have had 5 degrees added to allow for the magnetic variation. Even so, do not expect to be able to walk precisely on such bearings as paths always twist and turn and there are obstacles to go round.
6. All the routes were walked in 1993 and are as up to date as possible. However, conditions in the countryside change and not all changes are recorded even on the Ordnance Survey maps: forests are planted or felled, new fences erected, etc. Even if you find some variations from what is written in the text, these should not prevent you from finding a way round.

7. While every endeavour has been made to be accurate in all details, should some errors have crept in I can only apologise for these in advance. No responsibility can be accepted for any loss, etc. caused by an inaccuracy; and the fact that a walk is described in this book does not imply a right of way nor does it guarantee that access will always be available.

8. Feedback from the reader on changes that have been found, suspected inaccuracies or directions that do not seem clear, would be valuable and may be sent via the publisher.

ABBREVIATIONS

km	kilometres
ml	miles
m	metres
ft	feet
N, S, E, W	directions of the compass
NT	National Trust
NY, SD	National Grid reference
sp	signpost (-s, -ed)
TP	triangulation pillar
OL	Outdoor Leisure map

CUMBRIAN PLACE NAMES

In the ninth century England was attacked by what the Anglo-Saxons called Danes (to us the Vikings or Norsemen). They were a mixture of Scandinavian peoples who eventually settled north of a line from London to Chester and spoke Old Norse which scholars tell us was still similar to Anglo-Saxon. The languages blended, giving us many of the differences of dialect that still exist today and a large influx of vocabulary. The names of places were not always changed. Leeds, for example, is Celtic as is any hill with 'pen' in it, like Pendle. Many new names were of course created by the invaders (including the Norwegians who settled in Cumbria). A large dictionary will give the origin of many of these place names but a small section is given below:

bank	hill slope	keld	well, spring
beck	stream	kirk	church
birk	birch	knott	rocky hill
bottom	broad river valley	lang	long
by	settlement, farm	lath	barn
dale	valley	mel	sandbank or hill
esk	ash tree	mickle	great
ey	island	moss	marsh
fell	mountain	nab	rock projection
firth	estuary	rigg	ridge
foss/force	waterfall	scarth	pass, gap
garth	enclosure	slack	shallow valley
gate	road	thorp	outlying farm
gill	ravine	thwaite	clearing, meadow
hart	stag	toft	site of homestead
holm	island	whin	gorse
how	burial mound		

SYMBOLS ON SKETCH MAPS

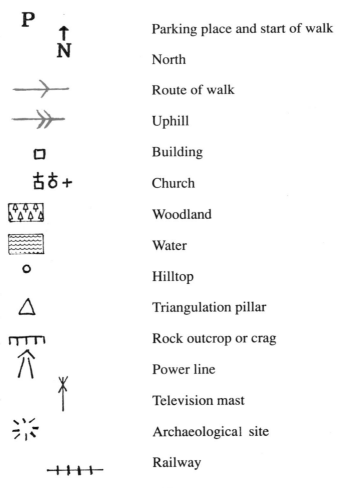

P
↑ N

Parking place and start of walk

North

Route of walk

Uphill

Building

Church

Woodland

Water

Hilltop

Triangulation pillar

Rock outcrop or crag

Power line

Television mast

Archaeological site

Railway

THE WALKS

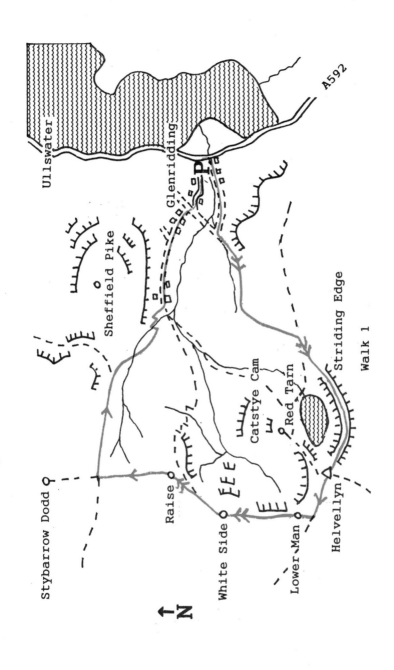

Ullswater

A592

Glenridding

P

Sheffield Pike

Catstye Cam

Red Tarn

Striding Edge

Walk 1

Stybarrow Dodd

Raise

White Side

Lower Man

Helvellyn

N

THE EASTERN FELLS

1. *Helvellyn by Striding Edge to Raise*

Ordnance Survey map no: 90/OL 5
Starting point: NY 386169
Walking distance: 17km/10.5ml
Amount of climbing: 990m/3,270ft

The ascent of Helvellyn by Striding Edge is a highlight for most walkers in the Lake District and it is highly popular. The actual crest of the ridge may now be bypassed on a path a few feet below and in wind this is certainly advisable.

There is a large carpark in Glenridding village with toilets and an information centre.

Return to the A592, turn right to cross the bridge and turn right again past a row of shops. Take the right fork to remain by the beck and just past a campsite turn left up a large track. Keep straight ahead through a gate sp HELVELLYN VIA MINES *(sic)* BECK. Go through the next gate sp HELVELLYN VIA MIRES BECK and turn left. A constructed path climbs by the beck as far as a wall which it follows until diverted to the right over boggy ground by a series of white-topped posts. It returns to the wall and reaches a ladder-stile. Cross this and the stile in the wall ahead (known as the Hole in the Wall) and continue on a large cairned path which leads to the narrow and exciting ridge of Striding Edge. After a last tricky chimney a short scramble leads to the Gough Memorial on the edge of the plateau. The shelter is a few hundred metres NW and the TP a little beyond.

Leave the summit on a bearing of 310 degrees with the

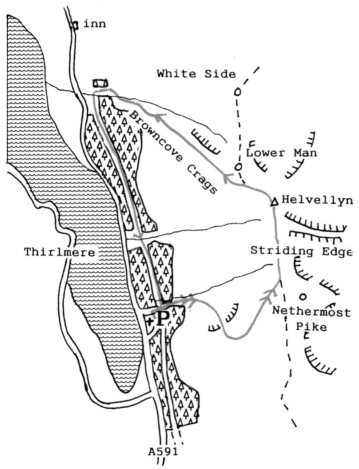

N

inn

White Side

Browncove Crags

Lower Man

Helvellyn

Thirlmere

Striding Edge

P

Nethermost
Pike

A591

Walk 2

steep escarpment on your right to reach Helvellyn Lower Man 1km away, forking right for the short ascent of 20m. Continue N down a narrow rocky ridge to a col and a short climb to White Side. The path to Raise goes NE but at the col take the path – not obvious in mist – branching left from the broad track which goes directly to Glenridding. From the rocky summit of Raise follow a cairned path down to a large col, Sticks Pass, and turn right, taking the path E down to some old mine workings. The path curves to the right by a group of five large cairns. Further cairns lead through the old workings and across a bridge. The path then zig-zags steeply down to a group of buildings. From here follow the rough road back to Glenridding, ignoring one fork on the left just before the first houses.

To shorten this walk continue on the path direct to Glenridding after descending from White Side. Save 1.5km/1ml.

2. Helvellyn from Thirlmere

Ordnance Survey map no: 90/OL 5
Starting point: NY 325136
Walking distance: 11.5km/7ml
Amount of climbing: 770m/2,550ft

Two of the easiest routes to Helvellyn are combined with a return on a forest track to make a good day out.

Park in Wythburn church carpark at the S end of Thirlmere on the E side of the A591.

Leave the carpark by a gate at the N end and follow a track uphill through trees by a beck at first. Cross a broad track by a sp (the return route is over a stile on the left). The track is cairned and well worn all the way to the summit. It goes up by Combe Gill before climbing right and then curving left. The angle eases off on grassy slopes and another track joins from the right at a col near the TP and shelter on the summit.

Begin the descent on a bearing of 310 degrees. A broad track soon emerges dropping to a small col. Fork left and go over the top of Browncove Crags. Below the crags the path follows an old wall before turning sharp left and passing a sheepfold and a large quartz rock. A ziz-zag track leads to

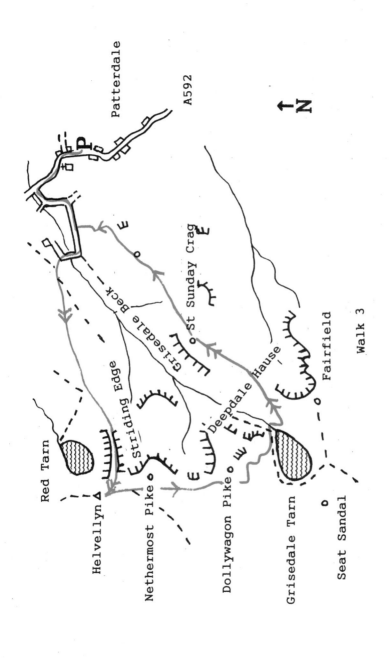

Patterdale

A592

N

St Sunday Crag

Grisedale Beck

Fairfield

Walk 3

Deepdale Hause

Striding Edge

Red Tarn

Helvellyn

Nethermost Pike

Dollywagon Pike

Grisedale Tarn

Seat Sandal

bridges and a gate to Swirl carpark.

By the exit to the carpark go through the gate on the left sp PERMISSIVE PATH TO GRASMERE. The broad track ends and is succeeded by a path waymarked with white arrows on blue circles, but now faded. Shortly after take the left fork. Cross a clear area with two bridges and rejoin the forest track. Cross the stile by a gate and turn right to descend to the carpark.

To shorten this walk retrace the route from the summit. Save 5km/3ml.

Walk 1, 2 and 3   On the summit of Helvellyn

3.   The Grisedale Horseshoe

Ordnance Survey map no: 90/OL 5
Starting point: NY 395160
Walking distance: 17km/10.5ml
Amount of climbing: 1,200m/3,950ft

It is difficult to know why this hasn't become one of the established Lake District rounds. It is certainly among the finest with an ascent of Helvellyn by Striding Edge followed by the long ridge of St Sunday Crag.

Park in the carpark in Patterdale on the E side of the A592 just S of the village school.

Turn right from the carpark, pass the church and go up a lane on the left just before a bridge. Keep on the lane as it

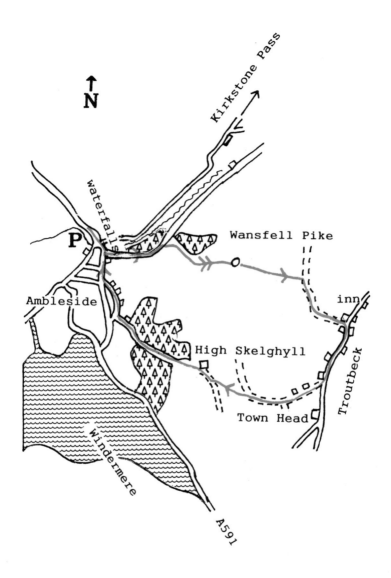

N

Kirkstone Pass

waterfall

P

Wansfell Pike

inn

Ambleside

High Skelghyll

Troutbeck

Town Head

Windermere

A591

Walk 4

turns sharp right at a crossroads of tracks. At a gate turn right, cross a bridge and shortly go through a stile and join a track going up left across the fellside. Fork right and you will soon see on the skyline the 'hole in the wall' to which the track leads. Cross the stile and follow massive cairns leading SW on to the narrowing ridge of Striding Edge. You can scramble on the top or take easier paths below, but all lead to a little chimney near the end. Go straight up the rocky face ahead to the Gough Memorial. The shelter and TP are minutes away to your right.

Continue by going S and forking left after 400m at a large cairn. The broad track takes you to Grisedale Tarn. As you descend, look on the opposite fellside for a path beginning at the outlet from the tarn and rising from right to left to a col. Cross the beck and climb this path, forking right in a shallow gully when near the col. Turn left over many false summits to the top of St Sunday Crag.

To descend, continue NE down several rocky outcrops to a grassy col where the path turns to the left flank of the fell. After an exposed traverse of the fellside cross a stile for the steep descent to the valley. From the next stile a gate can be seen to the left. Go through and turn right on your outward route.

To shorten the walk go directly down to Patterdale from Grisedale Tarn. Save 340m/1,100ft of climbing.

4. Wansfell Pike

Ordnance Survey map no: 90/OL 7
Starting point: NY 375047
Walking distance: 11km/7ml
Amount of climbing: 510m/1,700ft

This walk has one stiff but short climb which brings an outstanding view of Windermere. It is worth spending some time in Troutbeck including a visit to Town Head, a seventeenth-century yeoman farmer's house belonging to the NT.

There is a large carpark at the N end of Ambleside on the W side of the A591.

From the carpark turn right for the centre of Ambleside

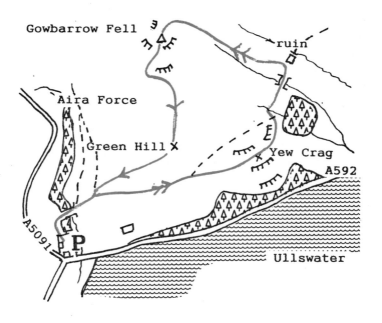

Gowbarrow Fell

ruin

Aira Force

Green Hill ✗

Yew Crag

A592

A5091

P

Ullswater

Walk 5

and turn left between Barclays bank and the Market Hall. (To
see Stockgill Force go into the park sp on the left and follow
the red arrows, returning to the lane through a revolving
gate.) Further along the lane climb an iron stile on the right
sp TROUTBECK VIA WANSFELL PIKE. A worn path leads
steeply to Wansfell Pike, the summit being on the far side of
a wall with a ladder-stile. Follow the cairned path E on a good
path. After the second gate turn right on an enclosed track
leading to the lane in Troutbeck. Turn right to continue the
walk or go left for the inn, the Mortal Man. At the post office
turn right up a stony lane sp BRIDLEWAY TO AMBLESIDE.
(Town Head is a few minutes' walk further along the lane.)

Turn left when you reach a gate sp SKELGHYLL, AMBLESIDE
VIA JENKIN CRAG. Descend to a surfaced farm road, turn right
and go through the farmyard on to a bridleway which leads
into woodland and past Jenkin Crag (viewpoint). Take two
right forks to stay on the main track and cross the beck. The
track becomes surfaced and drops down into Ambleside.
Turn right on Old Lake Road for the carpark.

To shorten this walk retrace your steps from Wansfell Pike.
Save 6.5km/4ml.

5. *Gowbarrow Fell*

Ordnance Survey map no: 90/OL 5
Starting point: NY 400200
Walking distance: 8km/5ml
Amount of climbing: 400m/1,320ft

A short walk giving outstanding views of Ullswater and the
hills around Patterdale.

Park in the NT carpark on the N side of the A592 near its
junction with the A5091.

Leave the carpark by a gate on the N side leading to Aira
Force, enter the wood and keep right to cross a footbridge.
Go up the steps, fork right and go right again to cross a stile
leading to a path on the open hillside. After 500m fork left
uphill on a path which then contours the hillside. Take the
right fork on the main path to reach a cairn above Yew Crag,
after which the path curves left, gradually climbing around
the hillside. Cross a footbridge, descend to the ruins of a

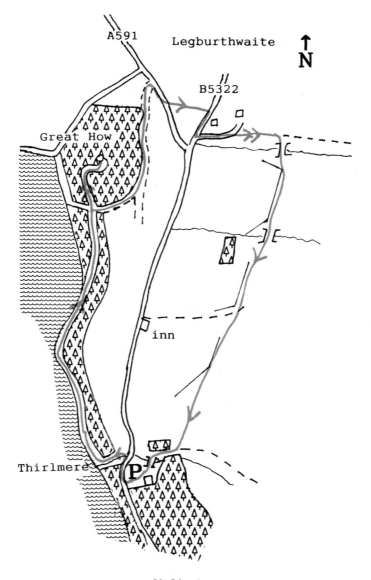

A591

Legburthwaite

N

B5322

Great How

inn

Thirlmere

P

Walk 6

shooting hut and turn left on a path now rising with a wall nearby on your right. The path goes through boggy patches and curves up left to a TP on a rocky knoll.

The next objective is a large cairn 1km to the S on Green Hill overlooking Ullswater but there follows a confusing area with many paths at first. Begin by leaving the TP on a bearing of 240 degrees then swing to the right around a crag and back to the left. Keep S on high ground and a more definite path appears. A cairn will be seen on the skyline from some distance. Turn right at the cairn on a green path leading down to a gate by the wood. Once through the gate, turn left for the carpark direct or right to visit Aira Force first.

To shorten the walk retrace your steps from Yew Crag. Save 4km/2.5ml.

6. *Great How*

Ordnance Survey map no: 90/OL 5
Starting point: NY 316169
Walking distance: 8km/5ml
Amount of climbing: 150m/500ft

A lovely walk which qualifies for this book by virtue of having one hill. The return traverse is superb and gives close views of several waterfalls – worth doing in the rain to see them in spate.

Park in Swirl carpark near the N end of Thirlmere on the E side of the A591.

Leave the carpark, turn right and cross the road into Station Coppice carpark opposite. Go through a gate sp LEGBURTHWAITE AND GREAT HOW. Follow the beck down to the lakeside, turn right and follow a route marked with white arrows, keeping on the path closest to the lake. After 2km take the direction sp Great How to the rocky summit.

Return to the sp and turn left to Legburthwaite. Turn left on a large track leading to the road. Cross with caution, turn right and cross a stile by a sp on the left, going over the field to a lane. Turn right, pass the youth hostel and go up a lane on the left sp GLENRIDDING VIA STICKS. Where the lane turns left cross the ladder-stile ahead and then a stile and gate to Beck Fall. Cross a bridge on the right and follow a sp to a

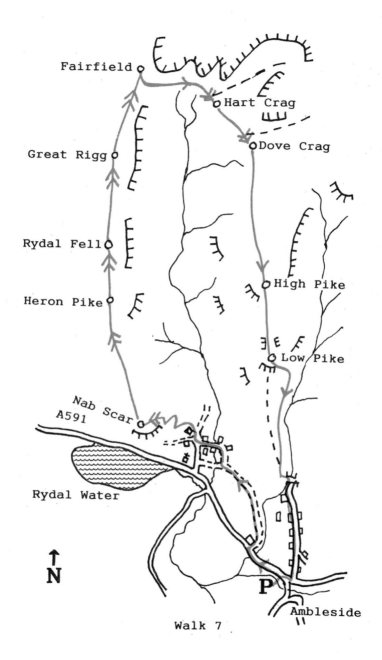

Fairfield

Hart Crag

Dove Crag

Great Rigg

Rydal Fell

Heron Pike

High Pike

Low Pike

Nab Scar

A591

Rydal Water

N

Ambleside

P

Walk 7

wall corner. Follow the wall until it drops right just before a small wood. Cross a bridge by a waterfall and follow the wall again as far as a fork in the track. Take the left fork across the hillside on a made track which gradually descends to the valley. At a track junction turn right and go through the trees to the carpark.

7. *The Fairfield Horseshoe*

Ordnance Survey map no: 90/OL 5 and 7
Starting point: NY 375047
Walking distance: 17km/10.5ml
Amount of climbing: 900m/3,000ft

This is one of the classic Lakeland horseshoe walks which stays at a high level for longer than most, giving outstanding views.

Park as for Walk 4.

Turn left from the carpark on the footpath along the A591 to Keswick and after 1km cross the road by a bus stop and go through an iron gate by a house on to a gravel track leading through parkland. Just before reaching a bridge turn right and follow footpath signs through a complex of buildings to reach a lane. Turn right, passing Wordsworth's home, Rydal Mount. Pass through a gateway and fork left on to a zig-zag path leading over Nab Scar and the ridge to Heron Pike, Rydal Fell and Great Rigg. The summit of Fairfield is over broad, grassy slopes beyond the ridge.

The route is now E but the first 100m are S. Follow a worn, cairned route which goes over the rocky area of Link Hause and then climbs on a bearing of 140 degrees to Hart Crag. (In mist be careful to take the right fork just before Hart Crag.) Descend to a col on 160 degrees where a wall is met. Follow the wall over Dove Crag and then down the ridge over High Pike and Low Pike. The main track then takes a broad sweep to the left away from the wall. If you miss this junction and stay by the wall you will have a slightly tricky little crag to climb down. Both paths meet on a stony track going down to Low Sweden Bridge. Go through a farmyard and on to a lane leading through the grounds of Charlotte Mason College and to the centre of Ambleside.

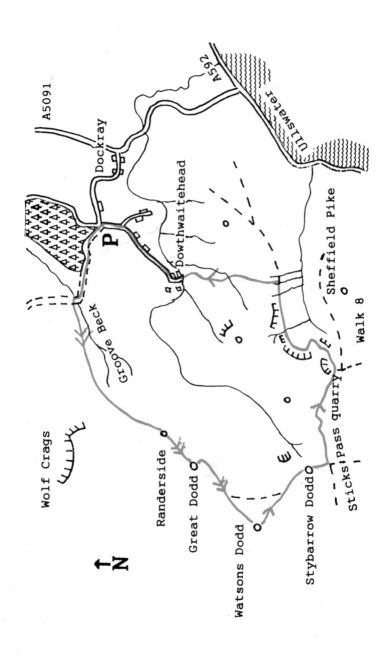

8. *The Dodds*

Ordnance Survey map no: 90/OL 5
Starting point: NY 380219
Walking distance: 15km/9ml
Amount of climbing: 750m/2,500ft

This walk offers good going on firm, grassy slopes with no steep gradients, plus an exciting high-level traverse. Only the descent to Dowthwaitehead is marshy. Difficult in mist.

There is ample parking at the junction 1.5km W of Dockray.

Go W along the stony track sp THRELKELD and after crossing the bridge/ford turn left up a wide path whose easy gradient follows the line of the beck until the ground levels and becomes marshy. The path is briefly less easy to see but keep towards the ridge ahead and you will soon be on firmer ground again with a clear path curving left to the cairn on Great Dodd, passing the rocky outcrop of Randerside. There is a shelter 150m SE of the cairn from which the path leads across the broad ridge. When this widens, curve right to the summit of Watsons Dodd which is on the W end of a plateau. From here go SE to Stybarrow Dodd.

Descend S to the cairn at the top of Sticks Pass and turn left on a path leading down to the spoil-heaps of old mine workings. You will reach five large cairns. Turn left here with no definite path but keep near an old quarry on your left. A cairn is reached by what looks like a sheep-track but which if followed will be found to curve around the hillside and then around the head of Glencoynedale as a magnificent high-level traverse almost Alpine in nature. Note on the far side of the valley a beck in a deep gorge and two smaller becks beyond it. Cross the large gorge and just above the next beck go uphill by a cairn to a broken wall where the ground levels out. The path down to Dowthwaitehead is difficult to locate but is on the left of the valley on a bearing of 20 degrees. Once found, it is thin but continuous until near a fence above the farm. Go through a kissing gate and cross the little gully to pick up a path to a footbridge and track to the lane. Turn right for the carpark 1.5km away.

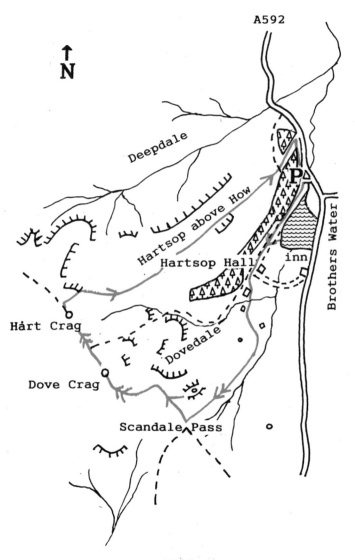

Walk 9

9. *Dove Crag and Hart Crag*

Ordnance Survey map no: 90/OL 5
Starting point: NY 403134
Walking distance: 13km/8ml
Amount of climbing: 820m/2,700ft

This walk gives good views of the craggy E face of the Patterdale fells. The gradual descent on a long ridge is one of the finest in the area.

There is a carpark by Cow Bridge on the W side of the A592. If it is full, try near the telephone box at Deepdale Bridge 1.5km further N.

Go through the gate at the S end of the carpark on to a stony track leading to Hartsop Hall. Pass Brothers Water and then, just past the farm, turn left over a bridge at a sp to Scandale Pass and Kirkstone Pass. Go through a gate and turn right on a track which turns left and crosses a bridge. Past the next barn follow the wall on your left and then continue to a gate. From here follow the path up to Scandale Pass and turn right, following a wall for a short distance and then a derelict fence. This goes NW at first before turning sharply W up the flank of Dove Crag. Although the fence meets the wall leading to the summit of Dove Crag it is convenient to turn right and cut the corner when the wall comes into view. The wall leads over Dove Crag and down to the col below Hart Crag. Maintain the direction for the summit.

About 50m beyond the summit turn right on a cairned path (bearing 60 degrees). Below the first short rock step the path divides. It is better to take the right fork to avoid an awkward crag. Continue along the narrowing ridge over Hartsop-above-How, the path being joined from the right by a wall which it follows. Just past a ladder-stile over this wall cross a ladder-stile over a cross wall and continue with the wall on your right down through a wood to a gate on the A592. Turn right and at once go up a short gravel path to a stile giving access to a path through the woods back to the carpark.

To shorten this walk turn right at the col between Dove Crag and Hart Crag and pick up a cairned path back to Hartsop Hall. Save 1km/0.5ml.

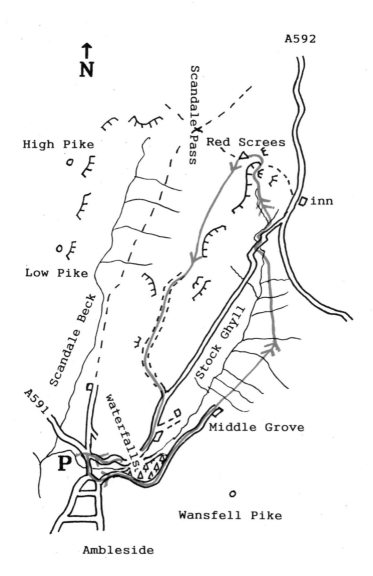

N

A592

High Pike

Scandale Pass

Red Screes

inn

Low Pike

Scandale Beck

Stock Ghyll

A591

waterfalls

P

Middle Grove

Wansfell Pike

Ambleside

Walk 10

10. Red Screes

Ordnance Survey map no: 90/OL 7
Starting point: NY 375047
Walking distance: 11km/7ml
Amount of climbing: 760m/2,500ft

This is an attractive walk, the ascent being up a valley and the descent by a long ridge. Care is needed on the broken rocks near the summit.

Park as for Walk 4.

From the carpark turn right for the centre of Ambleside and turn left between Barclays bank and the Market Hall. (To see Stockgill Force go into the park sp on the left and follow the red arrows, returning to the lane through a revolving gate.) Follow the surfaced farm road through the farmyard at Middle Grove on to the original rough, enclosed track. Continue past a ruined farm on a sp grassy path leading over a ladder-stile to a footbridge and a nearby gate. Turn right on the road and go through the second gate on the left visible 100m ahead. When you reach a crumbling wall turn left and follow it uphill until its remains turn to the right just below a small outcrop. Climb the steep grass to the left of the outcrop, at the top of which join a worn path coming from the inn. (To visit the inn continue past the crumbling wall and take the path from the NW corner of the carpark.)

When you reach the first short scree gully go up it, keeping to the right and making use of the rock until you are able to pull out on to a rocky rib which leads to more open ground. The path passes the head of a large gully. Take care here and scramble up, testing handholds as much of the rock is loose. A grassy area is reached and by bearing NW the summit is reached with a TP, shelter, cairns and a tarn.

The route off is SW on a well-worn path. Shortly after passing two large cairns, cross a decaying wall and soon another which the path follows down. Turn right on meeting a wall and cross a ladder-stile. The track descends between walls, aiming always for the head of Windermere. When the lane is reached turn right and descend to Ambleside and the carpark.

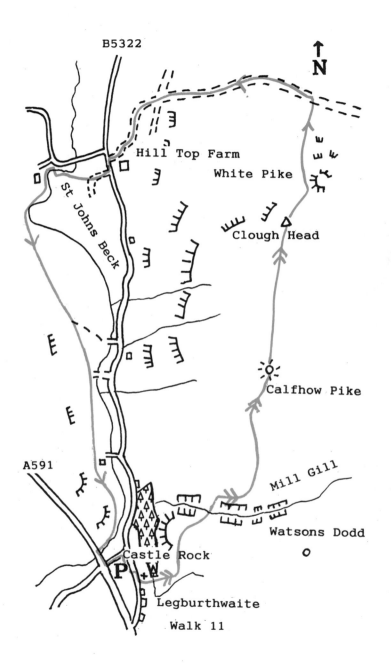

B5322

N

Hill Top Farm

White Pike

St Johns Beck

Clough Head

Calfhow Pike

A591

Mill Gill

Castle Rock

Watsons Dodd

P
+W

Legburthwaite

Walk 11

11. Clough Head

Ordnance Survey map no: 90/OL 5
Starting point: NY 318195
Walking distance: 13km/8ml
Amount of climbing: 650m/2,150ft

Clough Head is the most northerly peak of the Helvellyn range and its huge ravines are very impressive. Our route avoids them altogether but they are seen to good effect on the return along St John's-in-the-Vale.

Park in the water company's carpark N of Legburthwaite village on the W side of the B5322.

Go back to the road and turn right. Just past the chapel turn up left and go through a gate. At the top of the wood turn right and then left to follow the line of the beck uphill to a gap in a wall. Traverse the fell behind Castle Rock and at the next wall go half-right to find the only gap in the ravine of Mill Gill. Cross and follow the beck up until you are above the bracken line. Now work your way NE (no path) until you can see on the skyline the rocky tor of Calfhow Pike and make your way to it. A distinct path leads NE to Clough Head.

From the TP follow a bearing of 40 degrees along the ridge. Go to the left of the knoll of White Pike and down the grassy slopes towards a railway truck, to the left of which is a stile. Turn left on the old coach road, go over crossing tracks in the quarry area and left on the B5322. After 150m turn right on a sp track. When this turns sharp left, cross the stile ahead, go through a gate on your left, cross a bridge and turn left to follow the beck. A well sp route leads over stiles and up through a wood to the A591. Turn left and then left again down a disused road to the carpark.

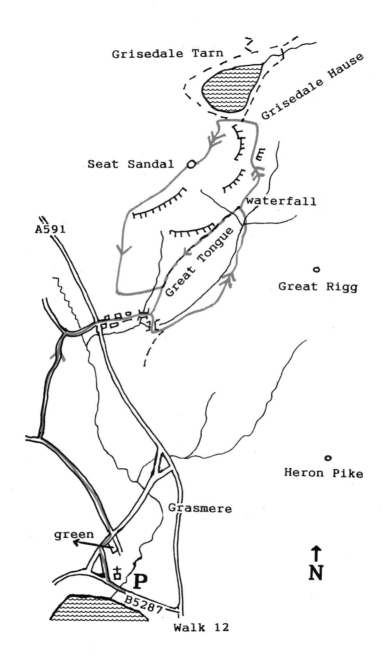

Grisedale Tarn

Grisedale Hause

Seat Sandal

waterfall

A591

Great Tongue

Great Rigg

Heron Pike

Grasmere

green

P

B5287

Walk 12

N

12. Seat Sandal

Ordnance Survey map no: 90/OL 5
Starting point: NY 339072
Walking distance: 12km/7.5ml
Amount of climbing: 635m/2,100ft

Seat Sandal dominates the E side of the Dunmail Raise and, being isolated, tends to attract only peak-baggers. The summit is a pleasant spot and the ridge route down is recommended.

Park in the carpark in Grasmere on the N side of the B5287 near the school. There are other carparks in the village.

From whichever carpark go N to find the village green and go along Easedale Road (following sp to Easedale Tarn). After 800m take a turning on the right sp to the youth hostel and after a further 1.2km turn right to cross the River Rothay and reach the A591. Cross and go up a track between houses sp to Patterdale. After the second gate cross a bridge or ford and then a smaller bridge on the right and turn left on a track, grassy at first. The forks in the track soon rejoin and the track goes above the wall, crossing a beck below large waterfalls and joining the track from Little Tongue. By a marshy hollow the path climbs over rocks on your left and reaches a wall with Grisedale Tarn beyond. Turn left, go 20m to bypass the rock and scree and then climb steeply on the grass, moving back to the left to reach an old wall which crosses the fell top within 30m of the summit cairn.

To descend, retrace your steps to the junction with the route up Little Tongue and fork right to reach the bridges and the outward route. If the weather is clear and you feel confident, descend the S ridge by making for a cairn at 250 degrees. There is no real path and cairns are infrequent, but keeping to the centre of the ridge leads down to a wall where a sp instructs you to double back sharply left and follow a path by the wall to reach the main track.

It is possible to shorten this walk by visiting Grisedale Tarn and returning by the same route. Save 1.5km/1ml.

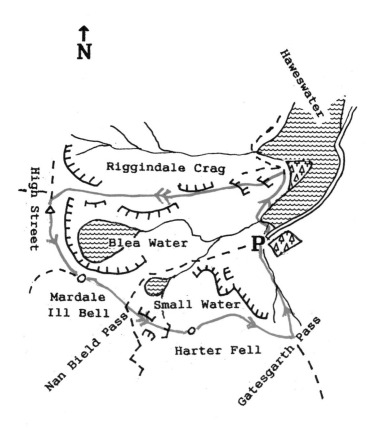

N

Haweswater

Riggindale Crag

High Street

Blea Water

Mardale
Ill Bell

P

Small Water

Nan Bield Pass

Harter Fell

Gatesgarth Pass

Walk 13

THE FAR EASTERN FELLS

13. High Street by Riggindale Crag

Ordnance Survey map no: 90/OL 5
Starting point: NY 469107
Walking distance: 11.5km/7ml
Amount of climbing: 820m/2,700ft

This is by far the most interesting ascent of High Street on a ridge which has on its northern crags the only breeding pair of golden eagles in England.

The small carpark at the end of the public road by Haweswater now has to be shared with eagle watchers, so come early.

Go through the gate at the end of the road and turn right at a sp to Bampton. The path goes round the end of the reservoir and above a plantation to meet a wall. Double back to the left on a good path which rises to the ridge and follows it to a short scree slope and a cairn on the plateau of High Street. Go half-left to a cairn from which you can see a wall and the TP. Continue S by the wall as far as a sheepfold on the W side and then go SE. You will pick up a worn path to Mardale Ill Bell from which it continues down to Nan Bield Pass, where there is a shelter, and up again to a plateau. (To shorten the walk descend N from the pass to Small Water. Save 1.5km/1.0ml.) Turn left for the summit of Harter Fell which is only 100m away by a fence corner. The route back follows this fence (NE at first) all the way down to a gate at Gatesgarth Pass. Turn left on a stony track to reach the carpark.

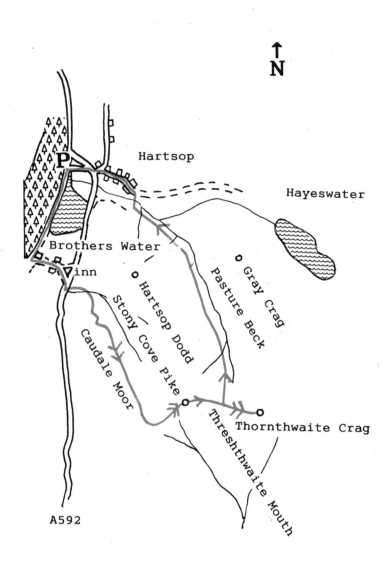

N

Hartsop

Hayeswater

P

Brothers Water

inn

Gray Crag

Hartsop Dodd

Pasture Beck

Stony Cove Pike

Caudale Moor

Thornthwaite Crag

Threshthwaite Mouth

A592

Walk 14

Harter Fell (Walk 17) from Riggindale Crag (Walk 13)

14. Caudale Moor and Thornthwaite Crag

Ordnance Survey map no: 90/OL 5
Starting point: NY 403134
Walking distance: 14.5km/9ml
Amount of climbing: 800m/2,650ft

The cairn on Thornthwaite Crag is a well-known feature in this area and is a worthy climax to a hard ascent.

Park as for Walk 9.

Go through the gate at the S end of the carpark on to the track past Brothers Water to Hartsop Hall. Pass the back of the farm and turn left to the access road which leads to the front. Pass through a campsite and Sykeside farm. Fork right to pass the inn and at the A592 turn right, crossing a sp stile on the left after 200m. Go up by the wall and take the zig-zag path to the ridge which leads to a wall. Turn left to a wall junction on the summit plateau, the highest point being on the E side of the wall.

The descent to Threshthwaite Mouth is over steep, broken rock which is dangerous if icy. A crumbling wall goes down and leads up again to Thornthwaite Crag. Return to Threshthwaite Mouth and descend N on the path above

43

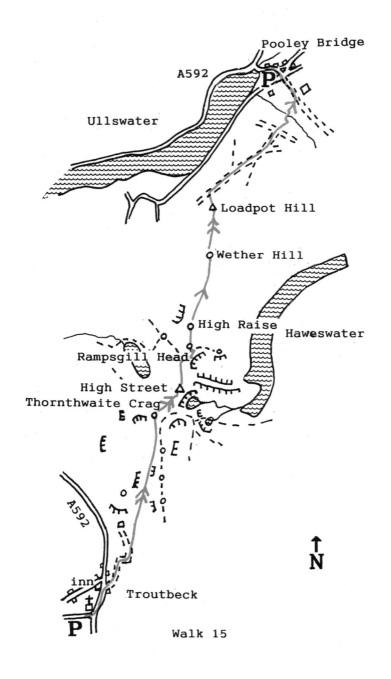

Pooley Bridge

A592

P

Ullswater

△ Loadpot Hill

○ Wether Hill

Haweswater

○ High Raise

Rampsgill Head

High Street △

Thornthwaite Crag

P

inn

Troutbeck

A592

↑
N

Walk 15

Pasture Beck. Cross a bridge, turn left through the carpark (alternative start) and follow the lane through Hartsop to the A592. Turn right for the carpark.

15. High Street Traverse

Ordnance Survey map no: 90/OL 5 and 7
Starting point: NY 412026
Walking distance: 24km/15ml
Amount of climbing: 970m/3,200ft

This is the only linear walk in the book and I include it partly because it is the best way to climb the fells concerned but mainly because it is among my favourites, a splendid high-level route along the line of the Roman road. Two cars are needed.

There is a parking area off a minor road just S of Troutbeck church. You will need to leave a second car in Pooley Bridge carpark (grid reference NY 470244).

Turn left on the A592, pass the church and after a further 500m turn right down a surfaced lane by the Queen's Head. Fork right and after 2km pass through a gate and turn right at a sp for High Street. Go through the gate on the fellside ahead on to a stony path. After passing two gates and reaching an open grassy area, fork right to a gate in a stone wall by a beck. A path goes up steeply and then crosses the fellside for 3.2km to the massive cairn on Thornthwaite Crag. Go NE on a wide path to join the wall leading to the TP on High Street. Follow the wall down to a col and at the top of the next rise fork right at a cairn. When the ground levels out turn left at a little cairn and a stone arrow to the top of Rampsgill Head and continue NE to the rocky summit of High Raise which is above the path to the right.

The route follows a wall and fence N; when these diverge it is better to stay on the higher ground by the fence until it turns away left. Pass through a gap in the wall, which is now just to the right, and over the top of Wether Hill. The path continues past the concrete base of a shooting lodge near the TP on Loadpot Hill. Continue N and just beyond the summit turn right on a large track. Go right at the first fork and left at the second and after crossing a marshy area go straight ahead

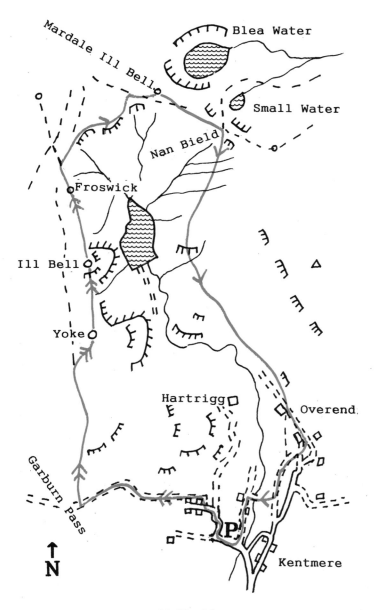

Blea Water

Mardale Ill Bell

Small Water

Nan Bield

Froswick

Ill Bell

Yoke

Hartrigg

Overend

Garburn Pass

N

P

Kentmere

Walk 16

on a fainter path at a crossroads of tracks. This leads to a beck which leads down to a ford. Beyond the beck the path turns left and then rises to a large, stony track where you turn left. This leads through a gate on to a farm road and then to a crossroads. Go straight over for Pooley Bridge and the carpark.

16.   Kentmere West

Ordnance Survey map no: 90/OL 7
Starting point: NY 456041
Walking distance: 16km/10ml
Amount of climbing: 820m/2,700ft

Serious erosion makes heavy going of the early stages of this fine ridge but is an indication of its popularity. An interesting traverse around the rim of the valley is followed by a gradual descent into the lovely Kentmere valley.

There is limited parking by the church. If this is full, drive further up the road; the last house on the left (double white gates) usually permits parking for a charity fee.

Walk up the lane, passing the fork on the right to Hartrigg farm and turn right at a sp TROUTBECK VIA GARBURN PASS. At the top of the pass go through a gate and turn right, following the line of a wall going N. Cross a ladder-stile and keep going N over Yoke, Ill Bell and Froswick, after which the path drops and begins to rise again. The next section is difficult in mist. Fork right at a cairn and take another right fork on a small, stony path which curves above the steep ground at the head of the valley and joins a larger track passing just below the summit of Mardale Ill Bell. Go up left for this peak and follow the path down to Nan Bield Pass where there is a shelter.

Turn right on to the path into Kentmere. This leads through fields and down to Overend farm where you turn left on a track. Just past some sheepfolds follow the bridleway sp to the right and cross a farm track on to a green lane which becomes walled. Watch on your right for a stone stile giving access to a bridge. Cross and turn left on another lane leading to the church.

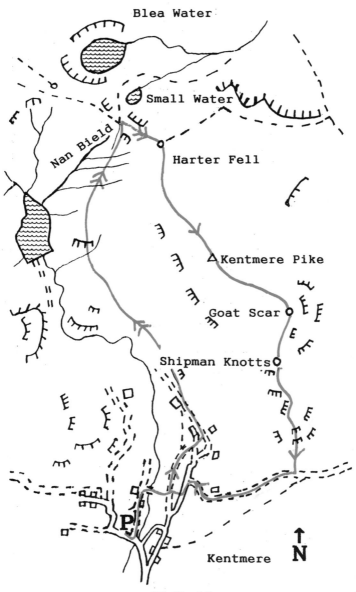

Blea Water

Small Water

Nan Bield

Harter Fell

Kentmere Pike

Goat Scar

Shipman Knotts

P

Kentmere

N

Walk 17

17. Kentmere East

Ordnance Survey map no: 90/OL 7
Starting point: NY 456041
Walking distance: 14.5km/9ml
Amount of climbing: 750m/2,500ft

This is the less popular side of the valley but is a pleasant walk nevertheless with good views into the unfrequented Longsleddale and good paths throughout.

Park as for Walk 16.

Go back past the church and turn left at a sp for Upper Kentmere and Kentmere Reservoir. Just past a house on the left go through a gate and cross a stone stile on the right to a footbridge and a stile on to another stony lane. Turn left and then follow the bridleway sp. At Overend farm turn right at a sp BRIDLEWAY MARDALE VIA NAN BIELD PASS. The path goes through fields and then zig-zags up to the pass where there is a shelter. Turn right for the short, steep climb to Harter Fell.

Follow the fence and then the wall S to Kentmere Pike where the TP is on the E side of the wall. Follow the wall/fence to a corner where the cairn on Goat Scar is 100m to your left, a worthwhile detour for the views. Keep by the

Walk 17   Harter Fell

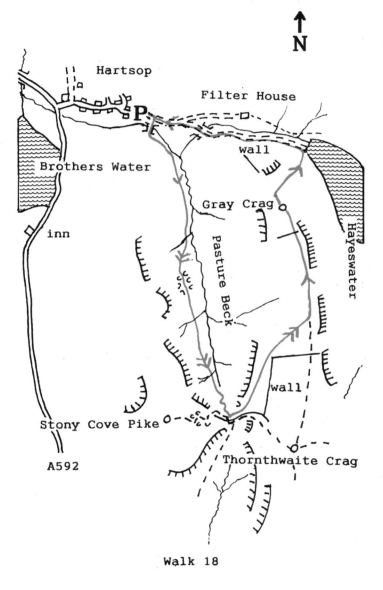

N

Hartsop

Filter House

P

wall

Brothers Water

Gray Crag

Hayeswater

inn

Pasture Beck

wall

Stony Cove Pike

A592

Thornthwaite Crag

Walk 18

fence to its junction with a wall, cross the ladder-stile and turn left to the top of Shipman Knotts. Follow the wall down to a pass, the last stretch being over some little rock steps. Turn right on a broad grassy track leading down to the road. Turn left and after 400m cross a stone stile sp on the right. Cross the stiles on each side of a track to reach a footbridge. On the far side of the river turn left on a track leading to the church.

18.   Gray Crag

Ordnance Survey map no: 90/OL 5
Starting point: NY 410129
Walking distance: 9km/5.5ml
Amount of climbing: 530m/1,750ft

Gray Crag is an agreeable, grassy plateau supported by broken cliffs with impressive downward views.

Park in Hartsop, NE of Brothers Water just off the A592. There is a small carpark at the E end of a narrow lane through the village.

Go through the gate at the end of the carpark, turn right at a sp PASTURE BECK and cross the bridge. The track follows a wall and then the beck before climbing high above it as a path leading to a wall across a col (Threshthwaite Mouth). Turn left and climb with the wall on your right until about 20m below a small crag on the right of the path where it is possible to leave the main track and turn left on the flank of the ridge. A small path very soon appears and leads to the corner of a broken wall.

Beyond this point the track peters out but go up right to the main track on the ridge. The summit cairn is just beyond another broken wall a little way off.

To descend, follow the track NW on the ridge. After an initial steep descent from the summit a path going E is met. Turn right on this and when it dies out continue to the N end of Hayeswater. Turn left and follow the beck with many waterfalls and pools back to the carpark.

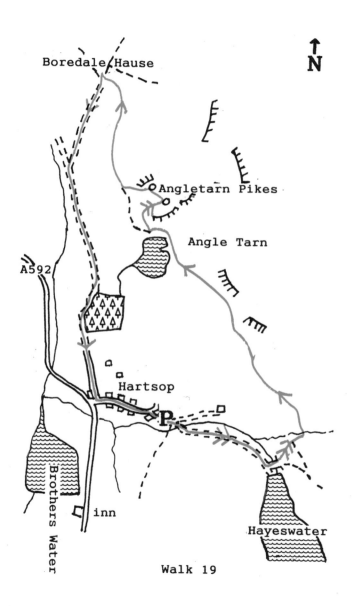

Boredale Hause

N

Angletarn Pikes

Angle Tarn

A592

Hartsop

P

inn

Brothers water

Hayeswater

Walk 19

19. *Angletarn Pikes*

Ordnance Survey map no: 90/OL 5
Starting point: NY 410129
Walking distance: 10km/6ml
Amount of climbing: 425m/1,400ft

A pleasant walk to distinctive rocky peaks overlooking an attractive tarn. A good high-level traverse follows.

Park as for Walk 18.

Go through the gate at the end of the carpark sp PUBLIC BRIDLEWAY HAYESWATER. After the next gate fork right, cross a bridge and climb by the beck to Hayeswater. Cross the bridge and take a track uphill going left. This peters out in a boggy patch but soon reappears as a grassy track and joins a wall. Follow the wall up to a junction with a track, turn left and cross a beck. The path traverses the hillside with a wall below and then a wire fence on the left before passing through a gate and descending to Angle Tarn.

At the far end of the tarn fork right on to the smaller track and curve around the fell before taking the easiest way through grassy rakes to two peaks. Return to the path which rejoins the main track dropping to Boredale Hause. At a flat, grassy area with a sheepfold take the left fork downhill going S. A track joins from the right near a wood. After crossing a footbridge go through a gate and continue between walls. The track becomes surfaced and joins the road to the village. Turn left for the carpark.

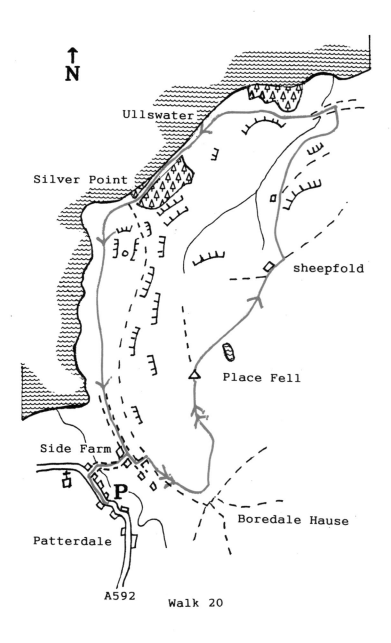

N

Ullswater

Silver Point

sheepfold

Place Fell

Side Farm

P

Boredale Hause

Patterdale

A592   Walk 20

20. *Place Fell*

Ordnance Survey map no: 90/OL 5
Starting point: NY 395160
Walking distance: 13km/8ml
Amount of climbing: 550m/1,800ft

Place Fell dominates the S end of Ullswater and is a most attractive fell with a broad top worth exploring once you are familiar with the basic route. The return by the lakeside is a real pleasure.

Park as for Walk 3.

From the carpark turn right on the road and right again just past the school on a farm track sp to Boredale Hause. Pass between the buildings of Side farm and turn right, then through a gate and turn left. Go right on joining a track across the fellside. Fork left to pass a seat and at Boredale Hause turn left on a path eventually going N to reach the TP on Place Fell. The path continues NE past a tarn and reaches a large sheepfold where you fork left. About 200m past an old quarry building fork left again and on joining a large track by a wall turn left on what becomes a lakeside path.

At the end of a bay is Silver Point and a small peak. Fork right here to keep by the lakeside and you will reach Side farm and your outward route.

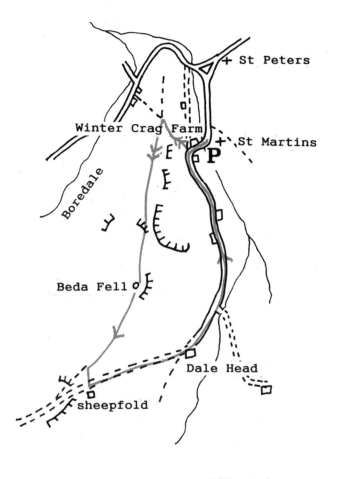

+ St Peters

Winter Crag Farm

+ St Martins

P

Boredale

Beda Fell

Dale Head

sheepfold

○ The Nab

↑
N

Walk 21

21. Beda Fell

Ordnance Survey map no: 90/OL 5
Starting point: NY 434184
Walking distance: 6.5km/4ml
Amount of climbing: 380m/1,250ft

This is a very quiet area with no through roads. A ridge path leads into the heart of the fells and an excellent track takes you back into the valley. Both churches on the route are worth visiting, St Martin's for its antiquity, St Peter's for its windows.

Park by Martindale Old Church which can be reached from Pooley Bridge – fork right past the village church and turn right at the crossroads. Pass St Peter's and take the next turning on the left.

Walk SW to cross the bridge, pass Winter Crag farm and look in the wall on the right, opposite the barn, for a slate sp FOOTPATH TO BOREDALE. Turn right. There is no path at first but one soon develops by a wall. On the crest of the rise turn left at the crossing track and climb the ridge S. The summit of the fell is the second cairn. Continue on the ups and downs of the ridge for a further 1.5km until you reach a small outcrop. Here fork left on a faint path which traverses the

Walks 21 and 22   The start

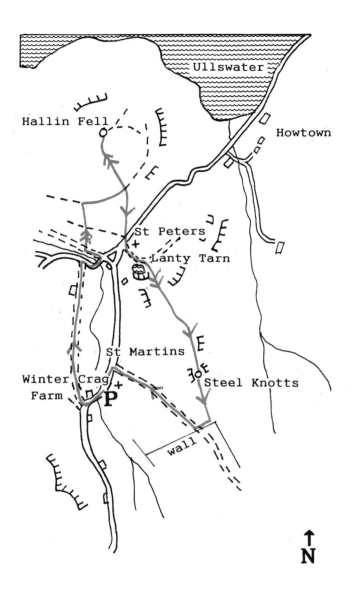

Ullswater

Hallin Fell

Howtown

St Peters

Lanty Tarn

St Martins

Winter Crag
Farm

P

Steel Knotts

wall

N

Walk 22

hillside for a few hundred metres and joins a large green track at a sheepfold. Turn left on this track which leads down to Dale Head farm and the lane back to the carpark.

22. *Steel Knotts and Hallin Fell*

Ordnance Survey map no: 90/OL 5
Starting point: NY 434184
Walking distance: 6.5km/4ml
Amount of climbing: 420m/1,400ft

Hallin Fell is very popular and the views of Ullswater from the obelisk are noteworthy. You will find fewer walkers on Steel Knotts.

Park as for Walk 21.

Walk SW to cross the bridge and just past Winter Crag farm turn right at a sp BRIDLEPATH TO SANDWICK, on a track between walls. Turn right at the lane, cross the bridge and immediately turn left on a stony track. After 50m take a path slanting up to the right. (Both the path and the wall above it are difficult to see when the bracken is high.) Cross a track by a gate and higher up fork right to stay by the wall before turning right on to another track across the hillside. This contours just above the wall and meets a broad, green path. Turn left on this for the summit of Hallin Fell and then return, descending to the lane. Cross and take the footpath past St Peter's church. After 100m this curves left by the usually dried-up Lanty Tarn. (Here there is a low concrete post.) Take a narrow path to the left of the small rock buttress in front of you and join a path going to the right of the crags higher up the fell. Follow the ridge SE and then go left to a cairn on the main ridge. Follow the ridge S to the rocky summit of the fell and maintain direction until a wall is reached. Turn right and follow the wall down steeply to a track about 10m below. The track leads NW down to the carpark.

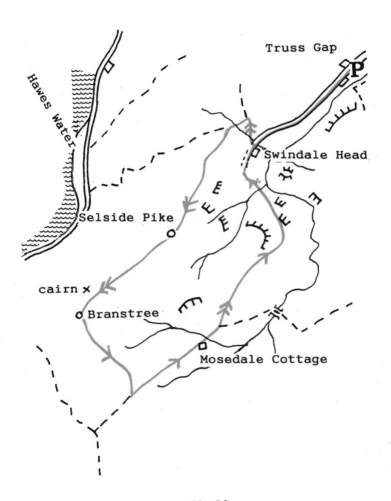

Walk 23

23. Selside Pike and Branstree

Ordnance Survey map no: 90/OL 5
Starting point: NY 515132
Walking distance: 13km/8ml
Amount of climbing: 485m/1,600ft

Solitude and outstanding views of the fells around Haweswater characterise this walk. The return is somewhat marshy.

There is a small parking area at Truss Gap. If this is full, there is another 1km back along the lane.

Walk W along the lane to Swindale Head, the end of the tarmac, where there is a sp for Old Corpse Road. A path rises steeply between walls and crosses a beck. Just above a junction with a wall from the right, fork left at a sp. The path now traverses the hill and re-crosses the beck before making for a guidepost on the skyline. Fifty metres beyond a second guidepost turn left on a faint path. This curves right and then left to reach the ridge where you turn right for the summit shelter by a fence corner. Continue by the fence (bearing 220 degrees) to Branstree. Note the superb cairn with its views of Haweswater on your right. The summit, a little further on, is merely an iron post, a few stones and a sunken TP.

Turn left to follow the nearby wall and then a fence down to a gate in a col. Turn left over boggy ground and a path emerges leading to Mosedale Cottage, a bothy with the optimistic slogan 'Home Sweet Home' on the door. The bridleway on your map starts off confidently but when a bridge comes into view on the right it fades and you must go uphill to the left to find it again. When you reach the head of Swindale the ground drops suddenly and the path fades again, but you can see it clearly below you to the left so head that way and the path is soon picked up as it winds its way through glacial moraines in a rocky amphitheatre with many lovely waterfalls. It leads to the farm at Swindale Head and the surfaced road back to the carpark.

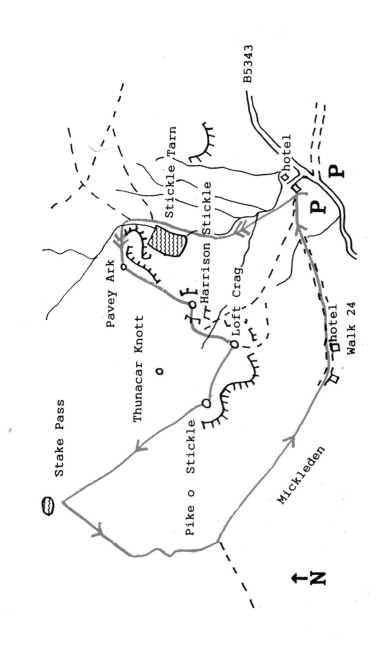

THE CENTRAL FELLS

24. The Langdale Pikes

Ordnance Survey map no: 90/OL 6
Starting point: NY 294063
Walking distance: 13km/8ml
Amount of climbing: 740m/2,450ft

The craggy profile of the Langdale Pikes, familiar from postcards and calendars, holds attractions for walkers and climbers alike. Route-finding requires care because of crags and it is not a walk to be done in bad weather.

Carparks are on both sides of the road near the New Dungeon Ghyll hotel.

From the NT carpark on the N side of the road go through a gate in the corner near the Stickle Barn. This gives access to the open fellside where a well-surfaced track follows the beck up to Stickle Tarn. Turn right along the E edge of the tarn and follow the beck uphill close to the crags, crossing it to go NW when the path forks. This leads into a stony rake, with crags on the left, to the top of Pavey Ark.

Go SW on a path around the rim of the crags to Harrison Stickle. Climb down the rocks on the W then follow a path which goes SW, crossing a beck to reach Loft Crag, and then NW along the edge of the crags to Pike O'Stickle. The scramble to its distinctive dome is reached across a grassy area.

The route is now NW over grass for 2.6km to Stake Pass. Just before a small tarn turn left on a track following a beck. Cross the bridge near a sheepfold and follow a stony track

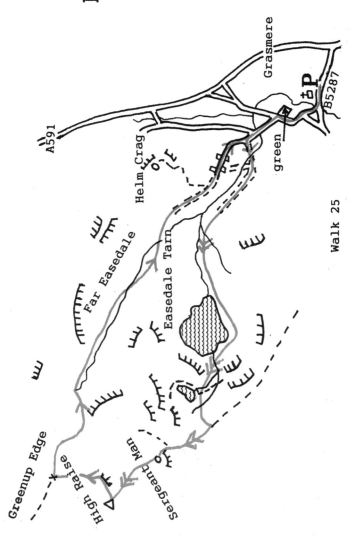

N

A591

Helm Crag

Grasmere

green

♿ P

B5287

Far Easedale

Easedale Tarn

Greenup Edge

High Raise

Sergeant Man

Walk 25

leading to the gate just above the carpark.

This walk may be shortened after climbing Harrison Stickle. Cross the beck and continue S and then SE down the ridge back to the carpark. Save 5.6km/3.5ml.

25. *Sergeant Man and High Raise*

Ordnance Survey map no: 90/OL 6 and 7
Starting point: NY 339072
Walking distance: 15km/9ml
Amount of climbing: 760m/2,500ft

An easily followed ascent via a popular tarn leads to a climb high among the hills with good views of the Langdale Pikes and central Lakeland.

Park as for Walk 12.

From whichever carpark go N to find the village green and go along Easedale Road (following sp to Easedale Tarn). After 800m turn left over a footbridge at a sp to Easedale Tarn. Fork left after a gate and follow the track up to the tarn. Walk to the W end on a path curving to the right over boggy ground before climbing steeply with some scrambling to reach a grassy hollow. Take a fork on the left to the top of the ridge. Turn right by numerous cairns at a track junction and reach Sergeant Man after a further 800m. High Raise is the

Walk 25   The approach to Easedale Tarn

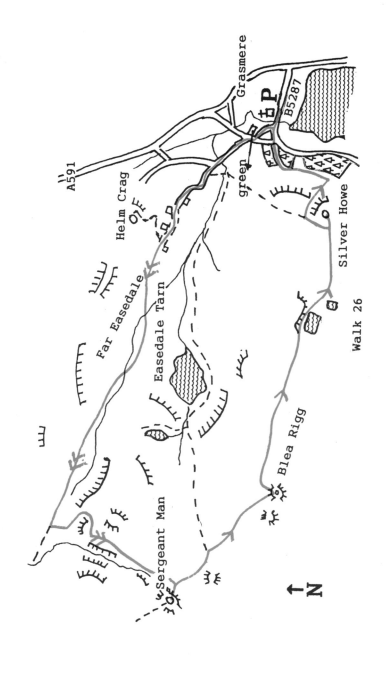

grassy mound at 304 degrees and its TP is reached in 10 to 20 minutes.

Descend by going to a second cairn at 40 degrees and then turning left to pick up a line of old iron fence posts going N down to the track over the col (Greenup Edge). Do not descend into the valley in front but turn right on the cairned but eroded track and follow it around the right edge of the hollow and up to a second col. Descend E into Far Easedale to reach Grasmere.

To shorten this walk retrace your steps from Sergeant Man. Save 1.6km/1ml.

26. *Sergeant Man and Blea Rigg*

Ordnance Survey map no: 90/OL 6 and 7
Starting point: NY 339072
Walking distance: 17km/10.5ml
Amount of climbing: 760m/2,500ft

The middle section of this walk, while not difficult to follow, is not on one of the main walking routes and is relatively quiet. The ridge from Sergeant Man to Silver Howe provides a long, high-level walk over easy ground.

Park as for Walk 12.

From whichever carpark go N to find the village green and go along Easedale Road (follow sp to Easedale Tarn). The road crosses a meadow and passes some houses before becoming a rough track leading up Far Easedale. The gill is crossed by a footbridge where the map says Stythwaite Steps and the track becomes a path leading up to a col. Here turn left on a bearing of 220 degrees and a small but clear path develops which follows roughly the line of old iron fence posts marking the former county boundary. The path swings left below a crag, back to the right above it and then follows the beck in a gorge below on your right. The fence posts should now be followed closely to a reedy tarn with the cone of Sergeant Man behind. Turn right at a track junction for the summit and then return to follow a broad ridge with many paths and tarns to Silver Howe, 5.6km away.

After passing the highest point of Blea Rigg there is a descent, and three tarns close together are passed. Nearer to

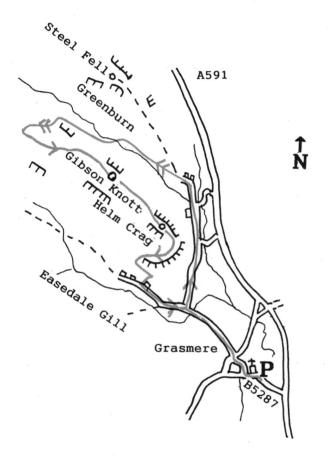

Steel Fell

A591

Greenburn

Gibson Knott

Helm Crag

N

Easedale Gill

Grasmere

P

B5287

Walk 27

Silver Howe the path passes above a large, reed-filled tarn with a gullery and two other tarns close by. Just after passing another tarn to the right the path rises to the grassy summit of Silver Howe. To avoid crags, retrace your steps and turn right to go around the summit knoll. Where the path forks, go to the right beneath crags and down a short scree gully, turning left on a track by the wall below. At the lane turn left for the village.

27. Gibson Knott and Helm Crag

Ordnance Survey map no: 90/OL 7
Starting point: NY 339072
Walking distance: 11km/7ml
Amount of climbing: 500m/1,650ft

The little Greenburn valley is among the less frequented in this area but it offers an easy route on a good path to the striking ridge leading to Helm Crag.

Park as for Walk 12.

From whichever carpark you use, go N in the village and along Easedale Road which runs from the N side of the village green. Just past the derestriction sign turn right at the sign for the youth hostel. Follow the lane for 1km and turn left immediately before a bridge. Cross the next bridge and at once fork left up a private gravelled drive sp FOOTPATH ONLY. Go through a gate just past the last house and up the valley with a wall on your left at first. Above the waterfalls and a dam a flat, swampy area is reached. Here the path turns left, crosses the beck by stepping-stones and continues past a sheepfold with huge boulders built into the corners. Continue climbing until a cairn in the middle of the path is reached. Turn uphill on boggy ground, still heading up the valley, until the path, now cairned, appears again. Near the ridge it disappears briefly again, and once more cairns guide you.

Once on the ridge the route is simply SE over Gibson Knott and, by a short scramble, to Helm Crag with the most wonderful views of the Vale of Grasmere. The path leads along the rocky summit ridge of Helm Crag and down to a grassy area where it turns right. It is now easily followed

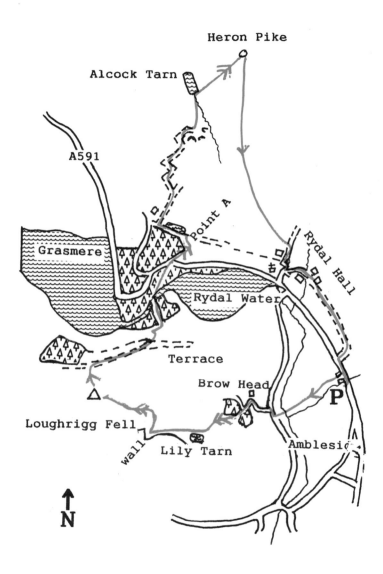

Heron Pike

Alcock Tarn

A591

Point A

Grasmere

Rydal Hall

Rydal Water

Terrace

Brow Head

Loughrigg Fell

P

wall

Lily Tarn

Amblesid

N

Walk 28

down, past a quarried area and between walls until it reaches the valley road where you turn left for Grasmere.

28. *Loughrigg Fell and Heron Pike*

Ordnance Survey map no: 90/OL 7
Starting point: NY 375047
Walking distance: 13km/8ml
Amount of climbing: 907m/2,993ft

Many unmapped tarns and footpaths make Loughrigg Fell difficult to navigate. The general direction of this part of the walk is NW. Heron Pike presents no such difficulties.

Park as for Walk 4.

Return to the A591 and turn left. After 50m turn left into Stoney Lane and at the end follow a footpath with a beck on the left. Cross the footbridge, turn right on the lane and after 50m turn left on a surfaced path sp to Loughrigg. On a bend take the footpath on the left sp to Clappersgate. Beyond a wood turn right (beck on the right). After 100m the path curves left away from the beck. Cross a stile and continue to Lily Tarn. Keep the tarn on your left and continue on a path from the NW corner. The path joins a wall and passes through a gate to join a green track after 100m. Turn left and curve to the right above sheepfolds. When the wall turns sharp left, maintain direction on a broad track N. Pass a cairn on your left and curve left under a small outcrop to climb W up a valley. At the head of the valley turn right on the main track leading NW to reach the TP after 1km.

Descend NW to a broad track at the foot of the fell – Loughrigg Terrace. Turn right. At a wall turn right and go through a gate on to a path through the wood. Cross a bridge and stay on the main path as far as a beck and footbridge. Turn left towards a toilet block and cross the A591. Take a path by a letterbox (beck on the left). The path turns to the right between walls, passes through the left-hand gate and joins a broader track (point A). Turn left. The track becomes surfaced and passes a reed-filled tarn. Turn right on to a stony track sp for Alcock Tarn. Go through a gate on the left on to a broad track. The path is vague at the top of Grey Crag – continue through a gateway in the wall ahead. Alcock Tarn

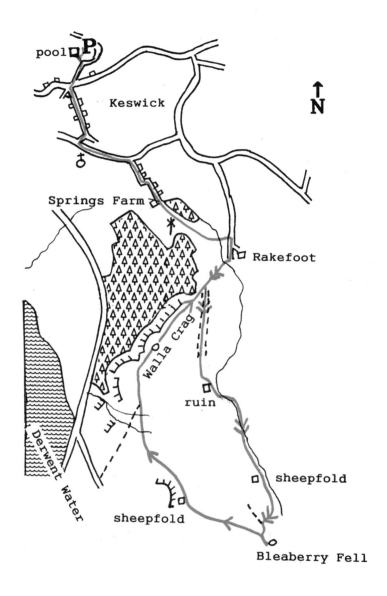

pool

P

Keswick

N

Springs Farm

Rakefoot

Walla Crag

ruin

sheepfold

Derwent Water

sheepfold

Bleaberry Fell

Walk 29

is 100m beyond. Cross the outlet of the tarn and cross a stile. Follow a bearing of 60 degrees to reach the summit of Heron Pike. There is no path but no difficulty. On the summit turn right and follow a well-worn path S and then SE along the ridge for 2km. At the foot of the fell turn right on a track with a wall behind. Turn left at a sp into the grounds of Rydal Hall. Cross the river and follow the sp between buildings to reach a broad track leading to the A591. Cross and turn left to Ambleside.

To shorten the walk turn right instead of left on the track at point A. This ends at a surfaced lane by Rydal Hall. Turn right and then left into the grounds. Save 4km/2.5ml.

29.   Bleaberry Fell

Ordnance Survey map no: 90/OL 4
Starting point: NY 270238
Walking distance: 12km/7.5ml
Amount of climbing: 560m/1,850ft

The outward leg of this walk appears little used, the path being thin and intermittent, but there are several landmarks to keep you on course. The contrast with the popular return route could not be greater.

There is a large free carpark by Keswick Leisure Centre well sp from the town.

Go round to the entrance of the swimming-pool and along Station Road to a crossroads. Cross by Corner House and go along Southey Street. Turn right at Church Road and left at Ambleside Road. Turn right along Springs Road and follow sp through Springs farm. Fork right at a sp before a footbridge, pass a TV transmitter, go through the gate ahead and cross a footbridge. Turn right on the lane and right again at a sp to Walla Crag. After the next footbridge and stile fork left on to a broad green track and when this forks go left, maintaining direction when the track peters out to reach some ruins and sheepfolds by some faint paths.

Turn left and follow the line of a beck all the way to its source, crossing as necessary and passing a sheepfold and then a short length of wall. Maintain direction on paths through heather, turning left on a green path and left again on

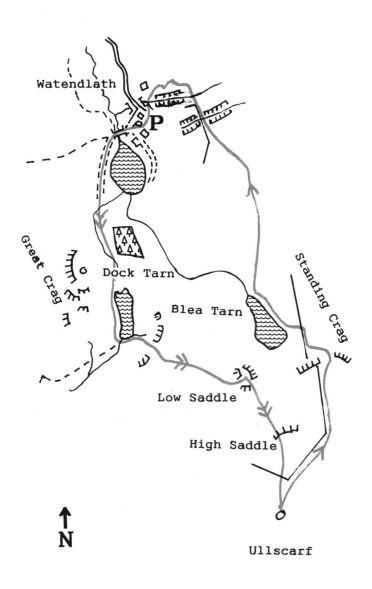

Watendlath

P

Great Crag

Dock Tarn

Blea Tarn

Standing Crag

Low Saddle

High Saddle

N

Ullscarf

Walk 30

a worn track to the summit.

Retrace your steps and follow the main track down, passing a sheepfold and crossing two becks before joining another broad track. Turn right and right again when a wall is reached. Cross a stile for Walla Crag and a scenic clifftop path. Leave by the stile and, with the wall on your left, rejoin the outward route.

To shorten this walk climb Walla Crag only. Save 5.6m/3.5ml.

30. Ullscarf

Ordnance Survey map no: 89 or 90/OL 4
Starting point: NY 276163
Walking distance: 12km/7.5ml
Amount of climbing: 500m/1,650ft

Ullscarf, not a peak of distinction, is considered the central point of the Lake District. Much of this quiet route is boggy and some of it is trackless so a clear day is essential for route-finding.

The NT carpark in Watendlath is reached by a minor road off the B5289 from Keswick.

Leave the carpark through the farmyard and cross a footbridge. Turn left and left again at a sp to Dock Tarn. The route is well marked, at one point by green-topped posts and stepping-stones over a boggy area. Go through a gate and up to Dock Tarn. One hundred metres beyond the S end of the tarn, the path turns right by a rocky knoll and is cairned. Turn left here, cross the beck and follow a narrow path, keeping near the marsh on your left (bearing 126 degrees). Climb a green gully half-right leading to a low col. At the top go slightly right to pick up a faint path. When this peters out head for the conical peak of Low Saddle on the skyline – there is no track, but take the safest route through boggy ground. From Low Saddle a bearing of 167 degrees leads to High Saddle and to a fence. Cross a stile, continue to the top of the rise and follow a line of old iron fence posts to the right to reach the small cairn on the summit of Ullscarf.

To descend, first return to the fence corner and then follow the general line of a fence on 60 degrees. After 1.5km the

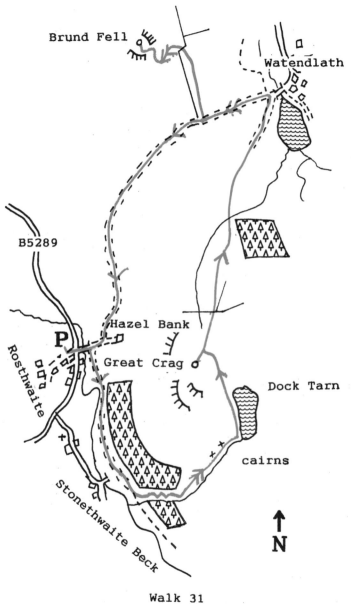

Brund Fell

Watendlath

B5289

Hazel Bank

P

Rosthwaite

Great Crag

Dock Tarn

cairns

Stonethwaite Beck

N

Walk 31

fence turns sharp right on top of Standing Crag. Curve right before this and go 150m to reach a gap in the crags before following the fence again. Turn left through the second gate and descend to Blea Tarn. Note a sp directing you to the right at the outlet to the tarn. The route is cairned and boggy but improves. Just above a farm, when the wall on the left ends, a well-paved track leads down to the carpark.

This walk could be shortened by visiting Dock Tarn and returning by same route. Save 7km/4.5ml.

31. Brund Fell and Great Crag

Ordnance Survey map no: 89/OL 4
Starting point: NY 258148
Walking distance: 10km/6ml
Amount of climbing: 535m/1,770ft

A riverside path is followed by a stiff climb to the secluded Dock Tarn overlooked by Great Crag. After refreshment in Watendlath the ascent of Brund Fell is followed by an easy descent by a bridleway.

Park in the NT carpark in Rosthwaite on the W side of the B5289, S of Keswick.

From the carpark return to the B5289, turn left and after 50m turn right at a sign for Hazel Bank Country House. Cross the bridge and turn right on the bridleway. Shortly after Stonethwaite bridge go through a gateway in the wall and turn left by a faded sp for Dock Tarn. A steep climb on zig-zag steps leads to the cairned path to Dock Tarn. Pass the tarn on your right and continue until the track turns right and is about to lose height. Turn left by a low wall on a crag, make for cairns through the heather and cross a gully to the cairned summit beyond. Retrace your steps to the track. Drop to a gate and follow green-topped posts and then a sp to a footbridge by the tarn. Turn right for Watendlath (toilets and café) or left to continue the walk. Where the track levels out, turn right, following a wall up to a ladder-stile. Cross and take a winding path up to Brund Fell. Retrace your steps to the track, turn right and descend to Rosthwaite bridge.

To shorten this walk omit the ascents of the two summits. Save 2.5km/1.5ml.

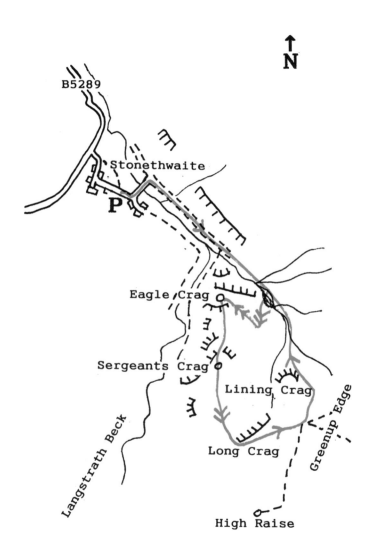

N

B5289

Stonethwaite

P

Eagle Crag

Sergeants Crag

Lining Crag

Langstrath Beck

Long Crag

Greenup Edge

High Raise

Walk 32

32. *Eagle Crag and Sergeants Crag*

Ordnance Survey map no: 89/OL 4
Starting point: NY 261138
Walking distance: 10km/6ml
Amount of climbing: 590m/1,950ft

The track in the valley is heavily used, not least by coast-to-coast walkers, but once it is left, this route is on the faintest of paths. It should not be attempted in poor visibility.

Park at a large roadside parking area just S of the village school in Stonethwaite on a minor road off the B5289, S of Keswick between Rosthwaite and Seatoller.

Continue S on the road and turn left just before a telephone kiosk, crossing a bridge and turning right on a bridleway. After 3km, past all the rocks of Eagle Crag, the beck divides into several branches and can be forded by an island with a sheepfold on it. Go up a grassy rakè slanting left and when above the bracken level turn right, making for a wall with a fence in front. At a point where there is no wall, the fence can be crossed without causing damage. Scramble up low rocks behind to the summit.

For Sergeants Crag go S from the summit to a wall corner. Do not cross the wall but climb down a rock step at the corner. Follow the wall at first and then swing away right on a faint path to the summit. Go S and cross a stile. Aim for the right end of Long Crag at the head of the valley. The faint path ends below the crags. Climb and turn left to cross the top of the crags and contour to the broad col of Greenup Edge where the main path comes up from Stonethwaite. Turn left and follow the cairns until a clear track leads down to the outward route.

To shorten this route retrace your steps from Sergeants Crag. Save 2.5km/1.5ml.

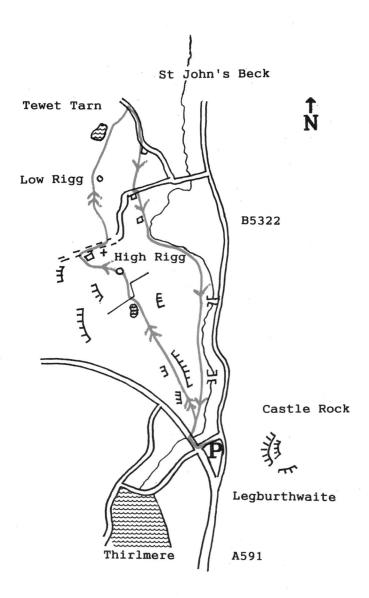

St John's Beck

Tewet Tarn

Low Rigg

High Rigg

B5322

Castle Rock

Legburthwaite

Thirlmere

A591

N

P

Walk 33

33. *High Rigg*

Ordnance Survey map no: 90/OL 5
Starting point: NY 318195
Walking distance: 11km/6.5ml
Amount of climbing: 320m/1,050ft

A delightful walk which has all the merits of the major fells except height. The return is through a pretty, pastoral valley.

Park in the water company's carpark N of Legburthwaite village on the W side of the B5322.

Leave the carpark at the N end, following a sp for a picnic area, and turn left on a disused road. Turn right on the A591, cross the bridge and a ladder-stile on the right and take a left fork uphill on a path winding over the highest ground. Go through a gateway in a wall and up rocks to pass a tarn on your left. The path swings left to cross a fence. Continue with the fence on your right to reach a small tarn. Descend, bearing left to reach a ladder-stile. Cross and continue with a wall on the right. When the wall turns right, maintain direction to the cairn on the highest point of the fell.

Descend by taking the easiest ground to the left and pick up a broad track through the bracken, reaching the lane to the left of a copse. Turn right on the lane and cross a stile by a sp on the left opposite the church. The track rises to a step-stile in a wall and curves around a knoll making for a gate and stile over a fence. Pass Tewet Tarn on your left and go over a stile by a gap in the wall. A footpath sp by the wall ahead takes you to the right, through a gap in the next wall and down to a gate on the lane. Turn right.

When the lane bends left keep straight ahead at a sp and follow a sp through fields to the next lane. Turn left and after 50m turn right at a sp and walk with the wall on your right over a stile and down to the river. Continue with the river on your left. A well sp route leads over stiles back to the bridge over the A591 (but do not take the one path sp on the left). Retrace your steps to the carpark.

To shorten the walk continue past the church after the descent from the summit and when the lane bends left keep ahead on the path leading down to the river. Turn right. Save 2.5km/1.5ml.

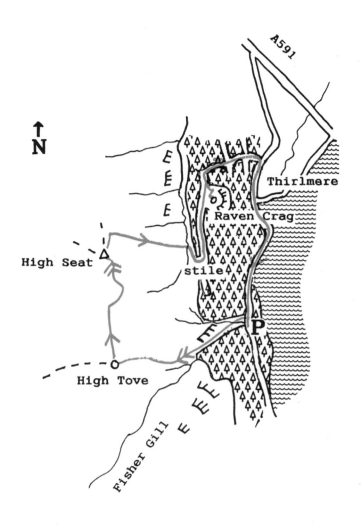

N

A591

Thirlmere

Raven Crag

E E E E

High Seat

stile

P

High Tove

Fisher Gill E E E

E E

Walk 34

34. High Tove and High Seat

Ordnance Survey map no: 90/OL 4
Starting point: NY 305171
Walking distance: 9.5km/6ml
Amount of climbing: 490m/1,600ft

There is some tricky navigation between High Seat and Raven Crag which adds to the challenge of this walk. This is a neglected part of Lakeland but one that all keen walkers will want to visit – but go in clear weather.

Use Armboth carpark off the minor road on the W side of Thirlmere.

Go up to the road, turn right and after 50m turn left at a sp footpath to Watendlath. This leads over to the forest edge on your left and beyond a wall on to a cairned path direct to the summit cairn of High Tove. Turn right and follow the fence which leads to High Seat. However, you will reach a marshy area and to get round this you must make an extremely wide detour to the right before reaching higher and drier ground again. At the top of the rise that has been in view, cross a stile to reach the TP on High Seat. Continue N, cross a stile not far off and go downhill as far as a junction with a fence from the left.

Here turn right on a bearing of 100 degrees, keeping to grassy or rocky knolls to avoid marshes. The ground drops away sharply when the forest comes into view and there are crags and a gorge. However, it is easily possible by working to the right to descend all the way to the beck on grass. Cross and turn right to a prominent ladder-stile that you will have noticed. Turn left on the forest track and follow it until you reach a large cleared area where a few metres to your right is a sp indicating Thirlmere to the E and Castle Crag to the W. Take neither but go up the unsignposted path through the trees to the top of Raven Crag with its splendid views. Return to the sp and turn right for Thirlmere. The path crosses two forestry tracks before reaching the road where you turn right for the carpark.

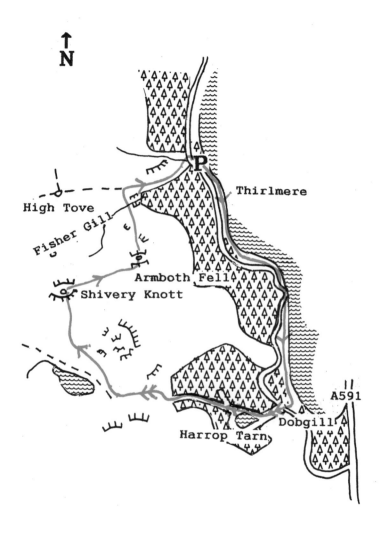

N

High Tove

Fisher Gill

Thirlmere

P

Armboth Fell

Shivery Knott

Harrop Tarn

Dobgill

A591

Walk 35

35. Armboth Fell

Ordnance Survey map no: 90/OL 4
Starting point: NY 305171
Walking distance: 12km/5.7ml
Amount of climbing: 380m/1,250ft

Armboth Fell was much maligned by Wainwright but no walker's knowledge of the Lake District can be complete without venturing on to this boggy central ridge. Go only if the weather is good as some of the route-finding is not easy. With the lakeside path this makes a good walk.

Park as for Walk 34.

Go up towards the road and through a gate on the left just before a cattle-grid. This gives access to a path wandering through the wood to Dobgill carpark, joining the road briefly by the viewpoint. Go through the carpark (an alternative start to the walk) and up a track sp to Harrop Tarn. Turn right on the lakeside path and left at a sp to Watendlath, following the blue arrows and then cairns to a clearer path. A double gate gives access to a path on the open moor. Turn left on joining another track which is cairned to a gate on the fence along the ridge.

Turn right and follow this fence, taking great care over the marshy ground. Skirt well to the right of a small tarn to reach a low, rocky knoll at the end of a second tarn. Beyond the next rise the fence turns sharp right and drops to a large outcrop (Shivery Knott). Here turn right and follow a bearing of 60 degrees to Armboth Fell which is 1km away. The summit is a small cairn on a large rocky mound.

To descend go roughly N downhill until you reach Fisher Gill. If you happen to meet it where there is a gorge do not attempt to cross but go uphill until the crossing is easy and continue on your original line. You will meet a cairned path. Turn right on this path which leads down to the road. The carpark is 50m to your right.

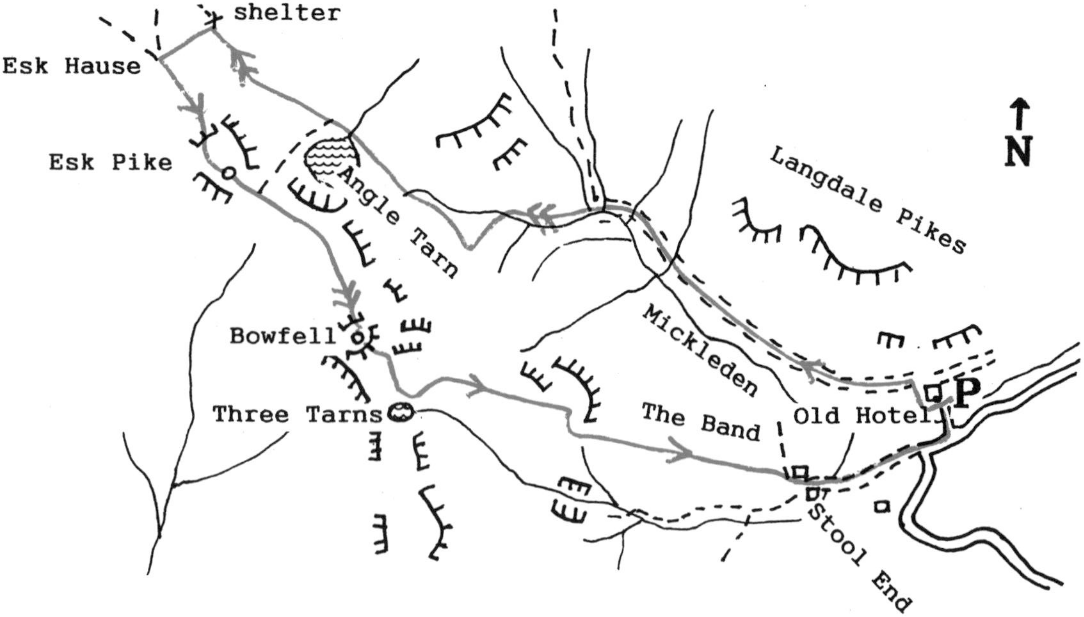

N

Langdale Pikes

P

Old Hotel

Stool End

Mickleden

The Band

shelter

Esk Hause

Angle Tarn

Bowfell

Three Tarns

Esk Pike

Walk 36

THE SOUTHERN FELLS

36.   Esk Pike and Bowfell

Ordnance Survey map no: 90/OL 6
Starting point: NY 286061
Walking distance: 13.5km/8.5ml
Amount of climbing: 970m/3,200ft

When combined in one walk, these two distinctively rocky peaks make a first-rate day in the mountains. The views of upper Eskdale on the approach to the Pike are unrivalled.

Use the NT carpark at the head of Langdale by the Old Dungeon Ghyll hotel. If this is full, use the larger carparks near the New Hotel and walk along the road to the start.

As you walk back towards the bridge turn right at a sp to Mickleden, Rossett Gill and Stake Pass. The enclosed path leads to a gate where you turn left on a stony track by a wall. The track goes up the valley for 3km with the Band on the left and the Langdale Pikes on the right. Cross a bridge near a sheepfold and fork left at the sp to Esk Hause. A path has been built which leads to rough ground in the bed of the gill and then to Angle Tarn. Just over the second rise a cross-shaped shelter is reached. Turn left to the slightly higher, broad col of Esk Hause, 250m away and turn left again to go SE to Esk Pike.

The route SE to Bowfell can be seen as a white scar in the rocks, dropping to Ore Gap and then curving S. As you scramble up the final rocks to Bowfell's summit note the cairns leading left towards the Great Slab which is the way down. Pass near the slab and follow cairns S to reach the pass

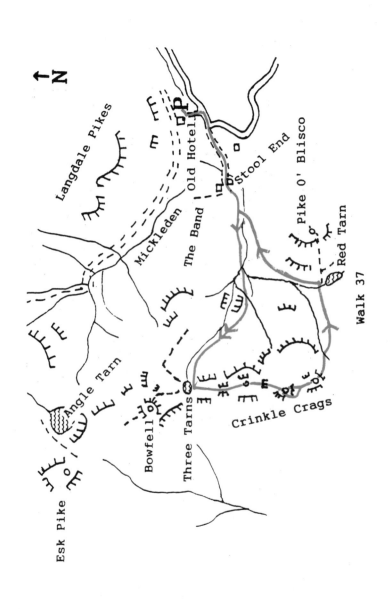

N

Langdale Pikes

Mickleden

The Band

Old Hotel

P

Stool End

Pike O' Blisco

Red Tarn

Walk 37

Esk Pike

Angle Tarn

Bowfell

Three Tarns

Crinkle Crags

called Three Tarns. Do not cross the beck but turn left to pick up the track on the broad ridge of the Band. This leads down to Stool End farm, passes through the farm buildings and along the farm track to the road. The carpark is just to the left.

37. Crinkle Crags

Ordnance Survey map no: 90/OL 6
Starting point: NY 286061
Walking distance: 13km/8ml
Amount of climbing: 805m/2,650ft

This is another classic Langdale walk with bare rock and steep gradients. Many parties have found the summit confusing in mist and it has the reputation of giving wrong compass readings. Tests showed that a compass laid on the rock could be inaccurate but otherwise was not likely to be.

Park as for Walk 36.

Return to the road and turn right. When the road turns sharp left keep ahead on the farm access road sp to Oxendale and the Band. Go between the farm buildings and through a sp gate to the left of the farmhouse. Go left at the sp for the Band and keep by the wall on your left to reach a gate and a track along the valley. Follow the sp through a sheepfold and pass a bridge. Where the wall turns up to the right you can continue by the beck but a better path is to be found by turning with the wall and then going to the left through the bracken. Both paths reach a bridge on the far side of which you follow the beck all the way up to its source at the pass, Three Tarns.

Turn left here and go S over the many ups and downs of the Crinkles by a worn, cairned path. From the summit of the highest Crinkle the main path goes to the left and comes to a gully with a chockstone. To the left of this the wall can be climbed down but it is certainly the hardest rock move in the book. There are easier ledges further left and it can be avoided altogether by going right from the summit on to a path making a wide detour. On top of the next and last Crinkle the path begins to curve left and becomes a broad track going E past a small tarn. (Near Red Tarn work has begun on rebuilding the path.) Just below Red Tarn cross the

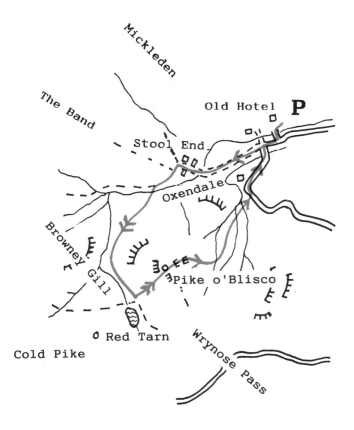

Walk 38

beck and immediately turn left on a path which leads steeply down the fellside to a bridge. Turn right on the far bank and reverse your outward route to reach the carpark.

38. *Pike O' Blisco*

Ordnance Survey map no: 90/OL 6
Starting point: NY 286061
Walking distance: 8km/5ml
Amount of climbing: 640m/2,100ft

This is a fine little peak with interesting rocky approaches all round and is a good excursion for a short day.

Park as for Walk 36.

Return to the road and turn right. When the road turns sharp left keep ahead on the farm access road sp to Oxendale and the Band. Go between the farm buildings and through a sp gate to the left of the farmhouse. Go left at the sp for the Band and keep by the wall on your left to reach a gate and a track along the valley. Follow the sp through a sheepfold and cross the nearby bridge with its memorial plaques. A path has been built up the steep fellside opposite and approaches Browney Gill which it then follows. Just short of Red Tarn turn left on a path going uphill. Near the summit this leads to a notch, the main cairn being to the left.

To descend, continue through the notch and pick up a path going E. Cairns lead over the rocks with four little chimneys to climb down, none causing any problems except perhaps the third which is narrow – tackle it on the outside. The path crosses a beck before beginning a steep descent down a gully over loose rock. The angle eases out, the rock gives way to grass and a track leads to the road. Turn left for the carpark.

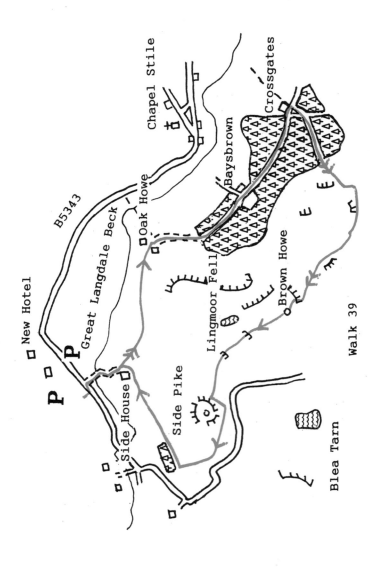

Chapel Stile

Crossgates

Baysbrown

B5343

Oak Howe

Great Langdale Beck

New Hotel

P
P

Side House

Side Pike

Lingmoor Fell

Brown Howe

Walk 39

Blea Tarn

N

39. *Lingmoor Fell*

Ordnance Survey map no: 90/OL 6
Starting point: NY 294063
Walking distance: 10km/6.5ml
Amount of climbing: 485m/1,600ft

The heather which gives this fell its name is on the northern end but it is attractive in many other ways, having woodland, tarns and crags. It also has many old quarries and was a major source of employment in the area.

Park as for Walk 24.

Go through the farm gate almost opposite the entrance to the NT carpark on the access road to Side House. The second gate on the left by the farm gives access to a footpath which rises and then contours the hillside. Turn right at a bridleway sp by Oak Howe cottage and follow this through woodland to Baysbrown farm from where it continues as a metalled lane, again in woodland. Just past Crossgates cottage turn right on a sp bridleway, go over a crossing path, through an old slate quarry and over a stile. At a little sign in front saying No Path turn sharp left on a path leading to a stile in a wall. This is now followed on your right along the ridge until it is succeeded by a fence. Fork right at a cairn to reach the highest point of the fell, Brown Howe, and continue with the fence on your left.

As you descend there are several little outcrops to go down, the wall reappears and is crossed again and you will reach a stile in a fence across your way. Behind it are the crags of Side Pike, unapproachable from here. Turn left and follow the fence down, crossing at the next stile on to a path contouring the fell. Stay on the path to a gap in the wall leading to a memorial seat and a path going NW over grass to the corner of a wood. Turn right along the edge of the wood, and keep on this path which brings you to the back of Side House. Cross the ladder-stile and turn left to reach your outward route.

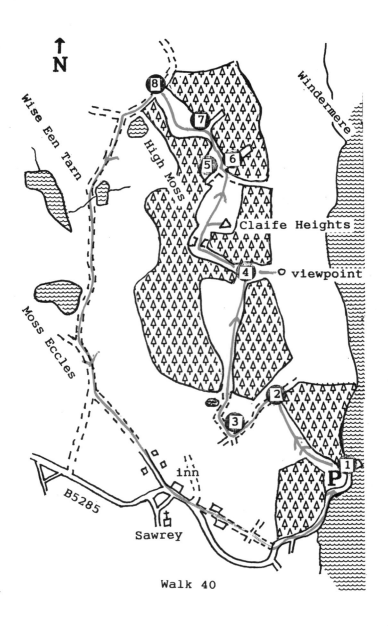

N

Windermere

Wise Een Tarn

High Moss

8

7

5 6

Claife Heights

4 ○ viewpoint

Moss Eccles

2

3

inn

B5285

Sawrey

1

P

Walk 40

40. Claife Heights

Ordnance Survey map no: 97/OL 7
Starting point: SD 388954
Walking distance: 10km/6ml
Amount of climbing: 290m/960ft

A walk noted for its views across Windermere and also of the peaks of Langdale from Moss Eccles Tarn. Some of the forest sections are being worked and are muddy.

Park at Ash Landing, NT carpark on the N side of the B5285 reached from Hawkshead and Sawrey.

The outward leg of the walk is marked by white-topped posts between eight sp with maps on. The sp are numbered on the maps and on the map in this book but do not themselves carry numbers. Start the walk at the back of the carpark by sp 1 (Claife Heights and Hawkshead), pass a ruin on your right and climb steeply. Go through a gate and turn left at sp 2. After 600m turn right at sp 3, pass a small tarn and enter a wood. Before turning left at sp 4, turn right for a viewpoint over Windermere. Follow the markers through the woodland, cross a footbridge and on entering a cleared area go up a rocky knoll on the right to a TP. Return and descend to a T-junction. Turn left to reach a forest road at sp 5, turn right and after 100m go left at sp 6 by a reedy tarn. Turn left at sp 7, and at sp 8 leave the white route, turning left on a forest road sp BRIDLEWAY SAWREY.

Turn left at a junction of tracks, with High Moss Tarn visible through trees on the left, pass between tarns and pass Moss Eccles Tarn on your right. Take the left fork sp to Far Sawrey and join a surfaced access road leading to the B5285. Turn left and past the inn take a lane sp to Ferry. Go through a kissing gate and keep close to an iron fence on your left before passing a riding centre on your right. Cross a drive and descend to the road again, turning left for the carpark.

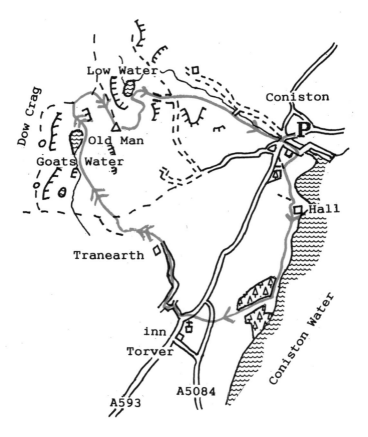

N

Low Water

Dow Crag

Old Man

Goats Water

Coniston

P

Hall

Tranearth

Coniston Water

inn

Torver

A5084

A593

Walk 41

41.   *Coniston Old Man*

Ordnance Survey map no: 96/OL 6
Starting point: NY 303976
Walking distance: 12.8km/8ml
Amount of climbing: 710m/2,350ft

This is a popular summit and none the less attractive for that but it is perhaps best kept for off-season. The route-finding is straightforward and the views are excellent.

There is a sp carpark in the centre of Coniston village. If this is full, park in the school grounds on Lake Road (fee payable; available weekends and school holidays only).

Turn left out of the carpark, cross the bridge to your left and go down the first road on the left (Lake Road). When the road turns sharp left go over a stile on the right sp to Coniston Hall and follow the field edge to the right. After a gate turn left at a junction of tracks by a wood on the right. A gravel track leads to a surfaced road where you turn left. Pass to the right of Coniston Hall and then go left towards a campsite. Take any path to the left leading to the lake and continue on the lakeside path over stiles to a wood and a sp to Torver Common. Keep by the lake as far as a clearing where you turn right at a sp to Torver. A stony track through the woods leads to a walled path, crosses a lane and an old railway line to the A593. Turn left and take the first turning on the right sp to Coniston Old Man and Walna Scar.

Further sp lead to a stony bridleway. This reaches a complex of sheep-pens through which blue arrows guide you over a bridge where you turn left on to a path between quarry spoil to the open moor. Pass a huge open quarry hole on your left and fork right further up. You will reach the Walna Scar track which you cross to enter a cwm. Pass Goats Water with Dow Crag on the far side and climb to a col (Goats Hause). Turn right on a broad track which gradually curves S to the TP, cairn and shelter on the Old Man.

To descend take the track at 130 degrees initially. This leads down to Low Water and then the quarry road back to Coniston. A better alternative is to keep straight ahead when the quarry road turns sharp right to go through a little pass.

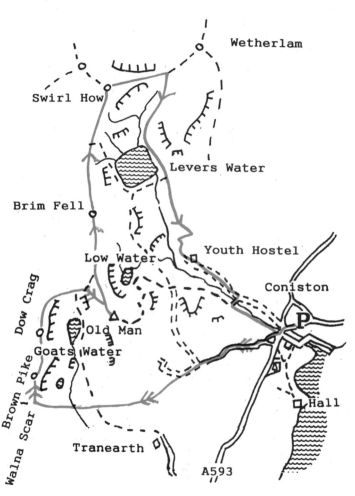

N

Wetherlam

Swirl How

Levers Water

Brim Fell

Low Water

Youth Hostel

Coniston

P

Dow Crag

Old Man

Goats Water

Brown Pike

Walna Scar

Hall

Tranearth

A593

Walk 42

This path passes the Miners Bridge and then the Sun Inn just before the bridge in the village centre.

42. *Dow Crag to Swirl How*

Ordnance Survey map no: 96 and 90/OL 6
Starting point: NY 303976
Walking distance: 16.8km/10.5ml
Amount of climbing: 1,000m/3,340ft

This is a more strenuous route than Walk 41 but is, again, popular and a good choice for low season.

Park as for Walk 41.

Turn left out of the carpark, cross the bridge to your left and go up the first road on the right sp to Walna Scar and Coniston Old Man. The surfaced section is very steep but eases off after a gate where the rough track leads up to the top of the pass. Here turn right on a worn path going over Brown Pike and Dow Crag and then down to Goats Hause. Continue on the broad path opposite curving S to the TP, cairn and shelter on the Old Man. (To shorten the walk follow Walk 41 down. Save 4.8km/3ml.) Retrace your steps but take a right fork to stay on the ridge and reach the fine cairn on Brim Fell. Drop to a col and climb a subsidiary summit to another well-built cairn on Swirl How.

The way down is by a path leaving the summit on 110 degrees. A narrow rocky ridge leads to a pass where you turn right. Pass Levers Water and the buildings in the valley. Cross the Miners Bridge on your right and continue on the far side of Church Beck. Just past the Sun Inn you reach the bridge where you turn left for the carpark.

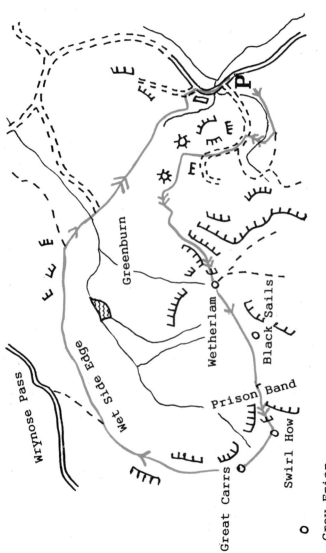

N

Wrynose Pass

Wet Side Edge

Greenburn

Great Carrs

Prison Band

Wetherlam

Swirl How

Black Sails

Grey Friar

Walk 43

43. Wetherlam to Wet Side Edge

Ordnance Survey map no: 90/OL 6
Starting point: NY 306009
Walking distance: 11km/7ml
Amount of climbing: 1,015m/3,350ft

A pleasant walk over rocks for the most part but with a superb grassy ridge towards the end.

Take the turning sp to Tilberthwaite on the A.593 N of Coniston. There are good parking areas on both sides of the bridge at Low Tilberthwaite.

Go up the sp steps at the S end of the carpark and join a broad track with Tilberthwaite Gill on your right. Fork right, descend to the bridge and climb the path on the opposite bank to a T-junction with a mine track. Turn left and fork right when the gill bends left. At a large cairn leave the track, keeping to the edge of a marsh on your right and making for a gap between two low hills. Follow a path going behind the left-hand hill and then contouring the fellside. The path curves slightly right to a stile and winds its way uphill to the narrowing ridge of Wetherlam Edge. From here scrambles follow SW to the summit.

The route goes W at first down to the col, Swirl Hause, from which a scramble up the ridge of Prison Band leads to Swirl How. The path to Great Carrs goes W but quickly turns N following the steep escarpment on your right. Just before the summit note the memorial cross and the bomber undercarriage. Cairns lead down through the boulders from the summit to a rocky track which is succeeded by the grassy ridge of Wet Side Edge. Two-and-a-half km from the summit a large cairn sits on the ridge. Fork right to reach the valley. The path continues E but when you are opposite the wall going up the fellside opposite turn right over boggy ground to reach it. Ford the beck (gaiters and stick useful) and follow this wall steeply up, crossing a stile at the top and keeping close by the fence/wall. Cross a stile and soon turn left on a larger track leading past cottages to the road. The carpark is 100m to your right.

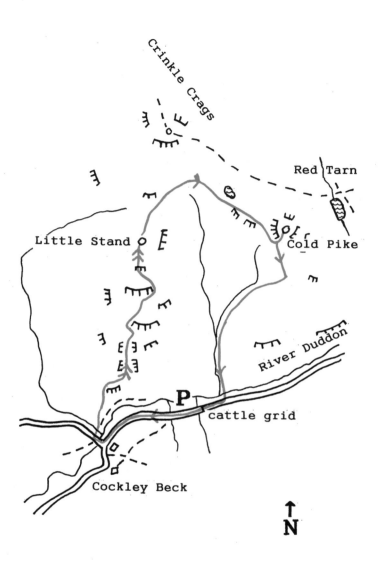

Crinkle Crags

Red Tarn

Little Stand

Cold Pike

River Duddon

P

cattle grid

Cockley Beck

N

Walk 44

44. *Little Stand and Cold Pike*

Ordnance Survey map no: 90/OL 6
Starting point: NY 255019
Walking distance: 8km/5ml
Amount of climbing: 550m/1,820ft

Although these peaks are in an area popular with walkers you will meet few others on them. As the route is almost pathless and with few landmarks, the description is of necessity generalised and this has the advantage of allowing you to make your own route over or around the many little crags.

The start is to the E of Cockley Beck Bridge. Park a few hundred metres to the W of a cattle-grid on a large, flat area near the beck on the N side of the road.

Walk W on the road and cross Cockley Beck Bridge with its gate. Turn right, ford the beck and cross a stile by a gate and sp. Follow the new wire fence to your right until you see a sheepfold on the fellside above. Begin now to go up left, keeping to drier ground along the bracken line on a path going over the lowest crag and then turning to go straight uphill to an old wall and a stile in the fence behind. Go right for a few metres and then go steeply up on a grassy tongue between crags. At a boulder-field detour right and rejoin it to reach a flat area bounded by crags. Work your way through broken rocks to another flat area, outflank the crags on the right and go up to the summit cairn of Little Stand. Keep going N towards Crinkle Crags, passing a marshy area on your right and dropping to a shallow pass. Turn right and curve around the head of the valley to reach a small tarn beyond which a faint path emerges going SE towards Cold Pike. Follow (if you see them) some white paint marks. Just below the summit there is a low crag which can be turned on the right.

To descend, first retrace your steps to the base of the low crag and in front you will see a line of white paint marks leading left. Skirt to the left of a marsh and keep following the marks. Head SW towards the trees by Cockley Beck Bridge. Just past the last of the marks a beck springs up. Keeping this on your right, use it as a guide to the valley

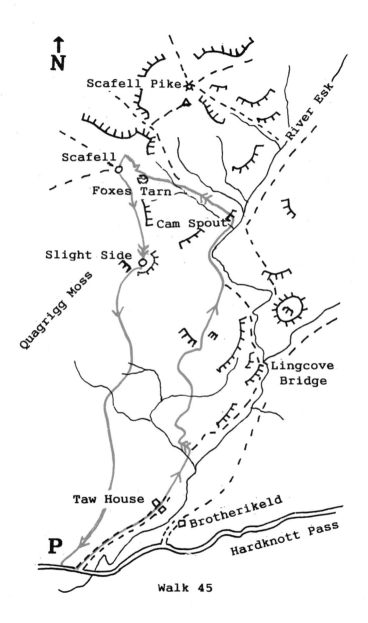

N

Scafell Pike

River Esk

Scafell

Foxes Tarn

Cam Spout

Slight Side

Quagrigg Moss

Lingcove
Bridge

Taw House

Brotherikeld

P

Hardknott Pass

Walk 45

where there is a gate. Ford the beck and turn right to the carpark which is a short distance away over the cattle-grid.

45. Scafell by Foxes Tarn

Ordnance Survey map no: 89/OL 6
Starting point: NY 201009
Walking distance: 15km/9.5ml
Amount of climbing: 940m/3,100ft

The base of England's second highest mountain is reached on this walk by a good path with easy going. There follows an adventurous scrambling route among high crags but with no inherent difficulty. The return is by the Terrace Route, not popular, but beautiful in its lower stages.

Use the small roadside parking area on the N side of the Hardknott Pass road to the W of Whahouse Bridge. The carpark is above road level.

Turn left from the parking area and after 100m turn left on a track sp to Taw House farm. Go through the farmyard on to a sp enclosed track. A path leads across fields to a bridge, immediately beyond which fork left uphill. A clear path winds up to a marshy area and curves around to the left to avoid it before coming back and bypassing High Scarth Crag which you will keep on your left. A cairned path leads through sheepfolds and continues to the right of some huge boulders before arriving at the foot of a waterfall (Cam Spout). Cross the beck and immediately scramble up the crags to easier ground above. Continue to a green amphitheatre and note the massive East Buttress of Scafell on your left. Do not go higher than its base but work over left to a small gully with a beck in it and scramble up from the cairn at its foot. You will reach the beautiful little Foxes Tarn, from the right of which a superb rock staircase has been built to the ridge. Turn left and you will reach the summit cairn and shelter in a few moments.

Make your way S to Slight Side, simply keeping the escarpment on your left. Just beyond its rocky summit the path turns to the right over scree and grass. From the bottom the route will take you down to the left of Quagrigg Moss. It will then constantly change direction but is excellently cairned and leads directly to a stile at the carpark.

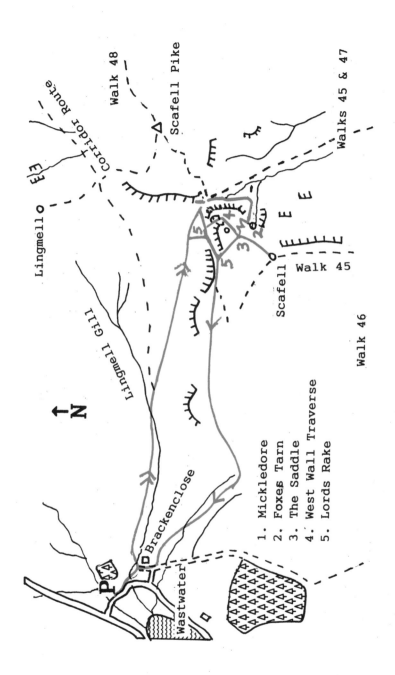

N

Corridor Route

Walk 48

Scafell Pike

Walks 45 & 47

Lingmell

Lingmell Gill

Walk 45

Scafell

Walk 46

West Wall Traverse

Lords Rake

Brackenclose

Wastwater

P

1. Mickledore
2. Foxes Tarn
3. The Saddle
4. West Wall Traverse
5. Lords Rake

Walk 46   Scafell Pinnacle

46.   Scafell from Wasdale

Ordnance Survey map no: 89/OL 6
Starting point: NY 182075
Walking distance: 8km/5ml
Amount of climbing: 900m/3,000ft

This walk takes you high among the crags of the Scafell
massif and offers several variations. All routes involve some
scree and scrambling.

Park in the carpark sp at Wasdale Head NT campsite.

Turn left from the carpark, cross the bridge and fork left.
Fork left again just before a stone building (Brackenclose).
Cross another bridge and follow a constructed path by the
beck. Fork right and reach a more level area with crags all
round. The direct route to Lords Rake and the West Wall
Traverse goes up scree to the right. For Foxes Tarn continue
up the steep scree and scramble to the col (Mickledore).
(Scafell Pike can be reached by turning left here on a worn
and cairned path.)

For Foxes Tarn go down the scree on the far side of the col,
working to the right beneath the East Buttress. About 100m
down scramble up a gully on the right marked at its foot by
a cairn. You will reach Foxes Tarn from which a constructed

107

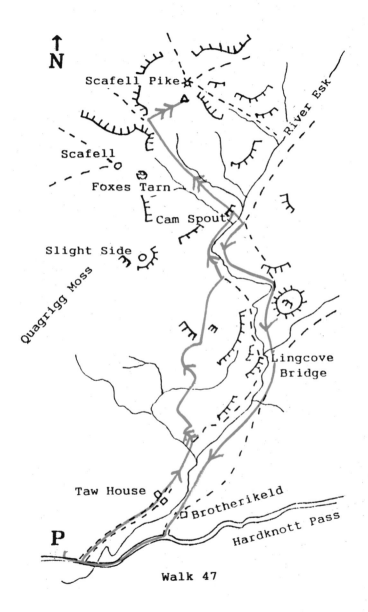

N

Scafell Pike

River Esk

Scafell

Foxes Tarn

Cam Spout

Slight Side

Quagrigg Moss

Lingcove
Bridge

Taw House

Brotherikeld

P

Hardknott Pass

Walk 47

path brings you to the saddle. Turn left for the summit.

For Lords Rake and the West Wall Traverse go to the S end of Mickledore and descend a steep path leading to a cleft rising across the crag; the direct approach joins at the foot of this cleft (Lords Rake). Climb it using the rock at the sides where possible. The cleft reaches a notch, drops and rises again to reach the main mass of the mountain. Turn left on steep, rocky ground to the saddle. Turn right for the summit.

The West Wall Traverse begins by going up Lords Rake. About 10m below the notch a narrow path goes left and reaches a huge gully (Deep Gill). Climb the loose rock to the plateau and turn right for the summit.

All routes return to the saddle; go downhill W and follow the edge of the escarpment by taking a right fork. Pass the exit of Lords Rake and continue down until grass is reached. At another rocky area past Rakehead Crag do not be tempted by the path which goes steeply down the rocky slope. Continue on the grass until the path turns to the right between two becks. Cross a stile over a fence and the gap in the wall behind it. Follow a grassy strip down and cross the beck to reach another stile. Turn right on the track by the wall below to reach the carpark.

47.   Scafell Pike by Cam Spout

Ordnance Survey map no: 89/OL 6
Starting point: NY 201009
Walking distance: 19km/12ml
Amount of climbing: 940m/3,100ft

A good path leads quickly into the heart of the fells. An adventurous route among high crags follows to reach England's highest mountain.

Park as for Walk 45.

Turn left from the parking area and after 100m turn left on a track sp to Taw House farm. Go through the farmyard on to a sp enclosed track. A path leads across fields to a bridge, immediately beyond which fork left uphill. A clear path winds up to a marshy area and curves around to the left to avoid it before coming back and bypassing High Scarth Crag which you will keep on your left. A cairned path leads

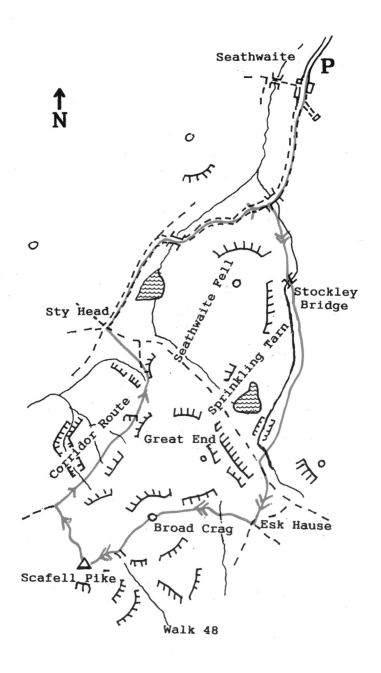

N

Seathwaite

P

Sty Head

Stockley
Bridge

Seathwaite Fell

Sprinkling Tarn

Corridor Route

Great End

Broad Crag

Esk Hause

Scafell Pike

Walk 48

through sheepfolds and continues to the right of some huge boulders before arriving at the foot of a waterfall (Cam Spout). Cross the beck and immediately scramble up the crags to easier ground above. Continue until you reach a col with a mountain-rescue box, the massive East Buttress of Scafell to your left. Turn right and follow a well-trodden and cairned path to the TP and the huge and recently rebuilt cairn on Scafell Pike.

Return by your outward route to the foot of Cam Spout but note that it is trickier in descent. Follow the beck to its junction with the River Esk which has to be forded – conditions are always changing. On the far side turn right and you will pick up a good path which follows the river (on your right) to Lingcove Bridge. Cross and turn right on a path leading through Brotherikeld farm and to the road. Turn right to reach the carpark.

48. Scafell Pike from Borrowdale

Ordnance Survey map no: 89/OL 4 and 5
Starting point: NY 235123
Walking distance: 15km/9.5ml
Amount of climbing: 850m/2,810ft

A relentless climb on rocky ground to England's highest summit is followed by a superb route traversing the mountainside. Good weather and an early start are essential.

Take the B5289 from Keswick and turn left into a cul-de-sac sp to Seathwaite. Park on the verge near the farm.

Walk through the farmyard, ignoring a sp on the right. Esk Hause, the first objective, is sp along a broad, stony track. After crossing Stockley Bridge, go through a gate and turn left, climbing with a wall on your left. The track leads in 2km to a level area with a huge crag behind. Cross the beck and turn left on the track, forking right after 300m to Esk Hause, a large, grassy plateau. At the cairn turn right on a track heading W. Follow the cairns through boulder-fields as the track curves SW to the huge circular summit cairn. Note that there are two descents of about 50m each between Esk Hause and Scafell Pike.

Descend on a bearing of 330 degrees but note that the path

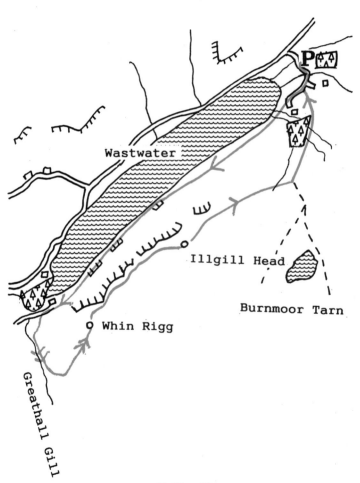

N

P

Wastewater

Illgill Head

Burnmoor Tarn

Whin Rigg

Greathall Gill

Walk 49

wanders right before leading to a large cairn on the skyline. A rocky path leads down until it forks just above a grassy area with a wall on the far side. The fork is not obvious but look for a line of cairns going right and follow them. This is the Corridor Route which traverses the fellside, crossing many becks and the heads of several ravines with an occasional scramble. Near the head of the valley take a fork left to the mountain-rescue kit on Sty Head Pass and then take the path NE past Sty Head Tarn. Cross a small bridge and follow the track down to Stockley Bridge to retrace your outward route.

This walk can be shortened by turning right at the top of Grains Gill. This will lead to Sty Head and the route down. Save 5km.

49.   *Whin Rigg and Illgill Head*

Ordnance Survey map no: 89/OL 6
Starting point: NY 182075
Walking distance: 14.5km/9ml
Amount of climbing: 530m/1,750ft

These are the two peaks that provide the rock for the famous Wastwater Screes. The route crosses the screes to begin with and you may debate whether this or the steep ascent that follows is the harder part of the walk.

Park as for Walk 46.

Go up the carpark track away from the road and turn right at a sp for Lake Shore. Cross the stile on the right before the farm to reach a grassy path which gradually crosses the scree. The really difficult section is right at the end and you should allow two hours to reach the pumping station. Follow the track and turn left at a sp TO FELL. The path follows a wall as far as the deep ravine of Greathall Gill where it turns left steeply uphill to the ridge and left to Whin Rigg. Several paths continue to Illgill Head but the best views of the crags are from a small path close to the escarpment on your left.

From Illgill Head continue NE on a good path dropping to a pass. An old wall is met and the first of many becks is crossed as the Corpse Road is followed left past some ruins down to the carpark.

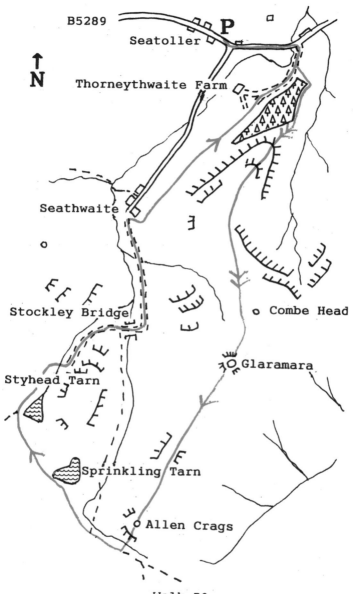

B5289

P

Seatoller

N

Thorneythwaite Farm

Seathwaite

Stockley Bridge

Combe Head

Glaramara

Styhead Tarn

Sprinkling Tarn

Allen Crags

Walk 50

50. Glaramara

Ordnance Survey map no: 89/OL 4 and 6
Starting point: NY 246138
Walking distance: 16km/10ml
Amount of climbing: 850m/2,800ft

A hard walk that takes you right into the heart of the mountains. From Glaramara's summit you can see both Windermere and Derwent Water.

Park in the NT carpark at Seatoller, on the N side of the B5289, S of Keswick.

From the carpark turn left and after 500m turn right on the access road to Thorneythwaite farm. Cross a ladder-stile on the left to join a well-worn path going by the edge of a wood, over open fellside and up a ridge to more level ground and a final scramble to the summit of Glaramara.

For Allen Crags continue SW on a cairned path winding over rocks and between tarns. A short descent leads to the main path from Langdale. Turn right, descending to Sprinkling Tarn and the mountain-rescue box on Sty Head. Turn right, pass Styhead Tarn, cross a footbridge and follow the track down to Stockley Bridge. Turn left for Seathwaite farm (café and toilets).

Just before the farm take a path sp to the right, go through

Walk 50   Great End and Ill Crag

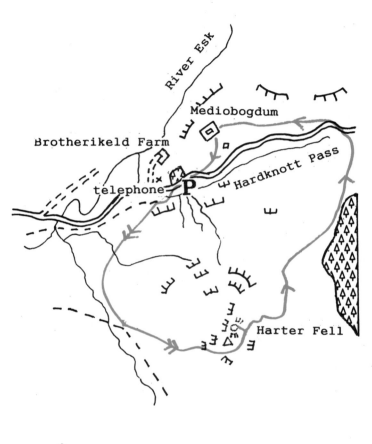

River Esk

Mediobogdum

Brotherikeld Farm

Hardknott Pass

telephone

P

Harter Fell

↑
N

Walk 51

a gate, follow a wall on your left, cross a field by cairns and again follow the wall. At the last field before the farm do not go through the gate but continue by the wall to the access road. Turn right to reach the lane and the outward route.

51. Harter Fell (Eskdale)

Ordnance Survey map no: 89 and 96/OL 6
Starting point: NY 214011
Walking distance: 9km/5.5ml
Amount of climbing: 575m/1,900ft

Harter Fell is a most attractive craggy peak, the summit being attainable only by a short scramble. If offers a superb viewpoint for the peaks of upper Eskdale and the walk finishes by going through the substantial remains of a Roman fort.

There is a small carpark just above the cattle-grid on the Hardknott Pass road E of Boot.

Cross the beck by the attractive footbridge and go through two kissing gates on to a green path rising across the hillside away from the wall. Go through two gates and continue with a fence on your right which the path leaves and then rejoins by a stile. Turn left here and follow a worn, cairned path winding uphill to a rock gateway. Turn left for the TP and summit.

Return to the rock gateway and turn left. The path twists among the boulders before curving left, heading for the end of the plantation ahead (bearing 40 degrees). The grassy slopes are thick with bog asphodel in July. Cross a stile and continue with a fence on your right. After the next stile the path swings away left through gaps in a broken stone wall and descends to the road by a section of Roman road. Turn left on the road but on the first hairpin leave it and make your way down on the right over grass to the Roman fort of Mediobogdum. From there cut across the bends in the road to reach the carpark.

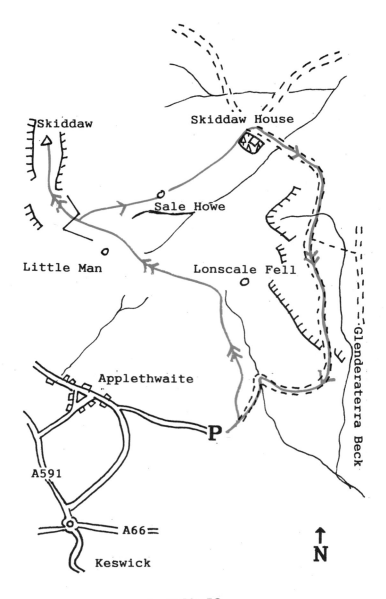

Skiddaw

Skiddaw House

Sale Howe

Little Man

Lonscale Fell

Glenderaterra Beck

Applethwaite

P

A591

A66

Keswick

N

Walk 52

THE NORTHERN FELLS

52. Skiddaw and the Glenderaterra Valley

Ordnance Survey map no: 89 or 90/OL 4
Starting point: NY 281253
Walking distance: 13km/8ml
Amount of climbing: 670m/2,200ft

The most popular route up Skiddaw is followed by a little-used route down. The finish is by a spectacular high-level traverse of Lonscale Fell.

There is a carpark at the head of a fell road reached from the A591 NW of Keswick. Take the road sp to Applethwaite and Skiddaw. Turn right at the T-junction and then left.

A sp footpath climbs between a wall and a fence. After the second kissing gate stay on a large stony track with a fence on your left at first. Pass through three gates before the final pull up to the TP and shelter on Skiddaw. Return to the last gate, go through and turn left. When the fence turns sharp left descend over grassy slopes on a bearing of 75 degrees and pick up a green track. This is not recommended in mist. The track goes to a col, over Sale Howe (cairn) and to Skiddaw House youth hostel.

Turn right, passing in front of the hostel and go through a gateway in the wall on to a track going SE at first. After 1.5km take the right fork going uphill on to a high-level route leading directly to the carpark.

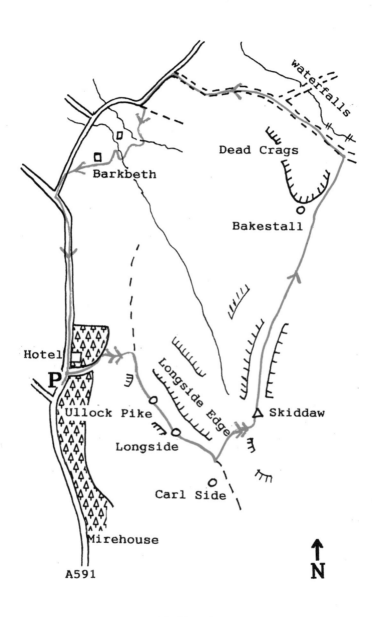

waterfalls

Dead Crags

Barkbeth

Bakestall

Hotel

P

Ullock Pike

Longside Edge

Longside

△ Skiddaw

Carl Side

Mirehouse

A591

↑
N

Walk 53

53. *Skiddaw by Longside Edge*

Ordnance Survey map no: 89 or 90/OL 4 (ascent only)
Starting point: NY 234294
Walking distance: 15km/9.5ml
Amount of climbing: 910m/3,000ft

An interesting and less frequented ridge leads to the summit
of Skiddaw, while the return to the N is also by lonely paths.
Not too difficult in mist.

Park in a lay-by on the W side of the A591, 7km/4ml W of
the junction with the A66 near Keswick, about 100m before
the Ravenstone hotel is reached.

Walk towards the hotel and cross the road to go through a
gate on to a bridleway. The path is very steep. Pass through
two more gates on to the open fellside. Follow the edge of the
wood on your left until, just before the brow of a rise, a cairn
indicates a stony path on the right leading to the ridge. The
path leads to a col and turns left across the flank of Skiddaw,
reaching the main ridge by a rough shelter. Turn left for the
summit with a TP and view indicator.

Descend on a bearing of 15 degrees. A track gradually
emerges and joins a fence from the right. Follow the fence to
its end where a short section of wall leads to a broad, stony
track. Turn left and left again when this joins a metalled farm
road. Turn left at a junction with a lane and at a right bend go
through a gate on the left. Take the right turn sp to High Side.
When the path turns right keep by the hedge to a gate with a
sp. Bear half-right and cross a bridge. Follow the track uphill
and after 50m double back to the left at a sp. Follow the sp
PERMISSIVE PATH with a wall on the right and turn right after
a stile. Cross a second stile and, maintaining direction, pass
the farm on the right to a further stile. Bear half-left to a gate
and descend to a lane. Turn left and left again on the A591 to
reach the lay-by in ten minutes.

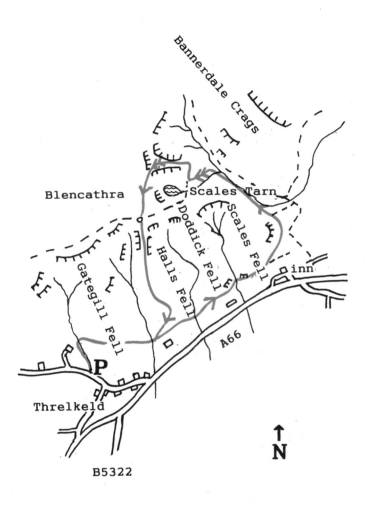

Bannerdale Crags

Blencathra

Scales Tarn

Doddick Fell

Scales Fell

Halls Fell

Gategill Fell

inn

A66

P

Threlkeld

B5322

↑
N

Walk 54

Walk 51   Harter Fell from Boot

54. *Blencathra by Sharp Edge*

Ordnance Survey map no: 90/OL 5
Starting point: NY 318256
Walking distance: 10.5km/6.5ml
Amount of climbing: 680m/2,250ft

On this walk there is a narrow ridge and a scramble to reach
the summit and a less spectacular but still steep and rocky
descent.

Park in the carpark in Threlkeld village off the A66. Turn
up a lane sp BLEASE ROAD LEADING TO BLENCATHRA

Walk up the path sp by the entrance to the carpark. Go
through a gate, turn right and follow a wall on your right for
3.25km, crossing three becks, the last with a scramble on
each side, before the path nears the A66. Just before a small
strip of wood on the right, fork left up a narrow stony path
which rises and turns left when Mousthwaite Combe is
reached. The path now traverses the hillside as far as Scales
Beck where it turns left. Near the tarn fork right and join a
gradually narrowing ridge. (To avoid Sharp Edge cross the
beck by the tarn and go to the summit by the clear path
ahead.) The scramble which follows up the main face of the

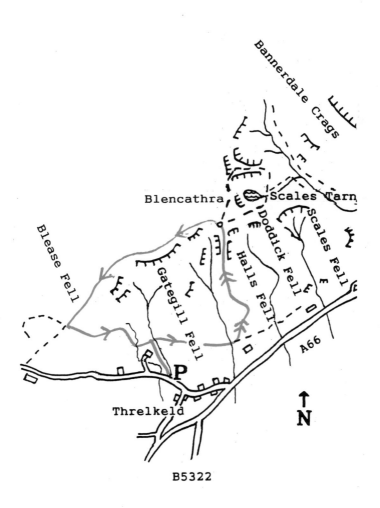

Bannerdale Crags

Blencathra · Scales Tarn

Blease Fell

Doddick Fell

Scales Fell

Gategill Fell

Halls Fell

A66

P

N

Threlkeld

B5322

Walk 55

mountain is possibly more difficult as most of the ridge can be avoided by using paths at a lower level. Turn left on the plateau to the simple summit cairn. Halls Fell, which is your way down, is directly in front of you on 160 degrees. It drops steeply at first and reaches the intake wall. Turn right and retrace your outward route to the carpark.

55. *Blencathra by Halls Fell Ridge*

Ordnance Survey map no: 90/OL 5
Starting point: NY 318256
Walking distance: 7.25km/4.5ml
Amount of climbing: 730m/2,400ft

This is a superb route to the summit but not as difficult as Sharp Edge. The descent is steeply over grass but easy.

Park as for Walk 54.

Walk up the path sp by the entrance to the carpark. Go through a gate and turn right, following a wall on your right as far as a beck. Ford the beck and fork left uphill on a zig-zag path leading on to the crest of the ridge and straight to the modest summit cairn of Blencathra. Turn left and continue over several small summits with the escarpment on your left. When the path begins to lose height it is cairned down to grassy slopes where it is still easy to follow. When you reach a broad, green path running across the hillside, turn left. This leads to further steep, grassy slopes down to a stile which you cross to continue with the wall on your right. Cross a beck and go through the gate on your right. Your outward route leads to the carpark.

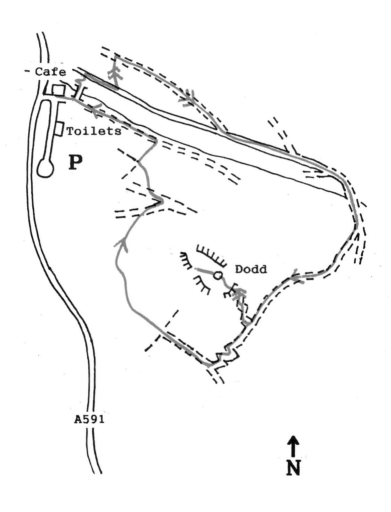

Cafe

Toilets

P

Dodd

A591

↑
N

Walk 56

56.   Dodd

Ordnance Survey map no: 89 or 90/OL 4
Starting point: NY 235281
Walking distance: 5km/3ml
Amount of climbing: 400m/1,320ft

The most interesting route to the summit of Dodd is now marked by the Forestry Commission on posts with a green band. A good short walk at any time of year.

Park at the Forestry Commission centre at Mirehouse off the A591, 5km/3ml NW of the junction with the A66 near Keswick.

From the café go uphill, following the route markers over a bridge. Zig-zag up to a metalled forestry road and turn right. After 400m turn left up a small path with sp 4 above. A short climb leads to a forest track – turn right following the red/green markers. On rejoining the metalled forest road, turn left (green markers only). Maintain direction when another forest track joins from the left. Take a fork right sp to Dodd Summit and shortly after go right again at a sp reading Dodd Summit 300m. Pass a memorial to the Scouts to reach the viewpoint.

Retrace your steps to the forest track and turn right. The track zig-zags and continues down to a crossroads. Go straight over into the wood on a small path. At a forest track turn right and after 20m go left at a junction. After 100m fork right on a path. Turn right at a path crossing and after 20m turn left and follow the beck to the carpark.

Note: The whole area is forest in various and changing stages of growth. On the map all trees have been omitted for clarity.

This walk could be shortened by following the red markers. Save 2.5km/1.5ml.

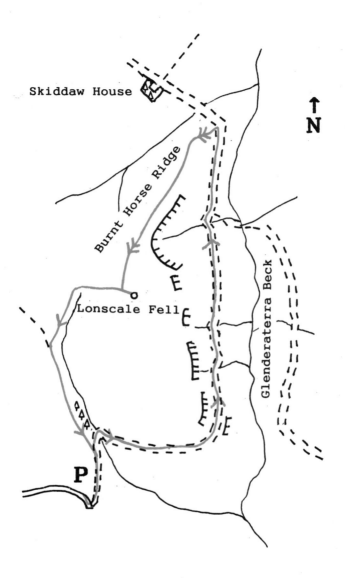

Skiddaw House

Burnt Horse Ridge

Lonscale Fell

Glenderaterra Beck

P

N

Walk 57

57.   Lonscale Fell

Ordnance Survey map no: 90/OL 4
Starting point: NY 281253
Walking distance: 9.5km/6ml
Amount of climbing: 420m/1,400ft

A carpark at 300m/1,000ft makes the attainment of this peak relatively easy. The walk up the valley must rate as one of the best high-level routes in the area.

Park as for Walk 52.

Cross the sp stile at the S end of the carpark on to a fenced-in path. At the end of this, fork right on a track traversing the fellside until after 5km you reach a gate. Turn left and follow the wall/fence up to a gate on the fell top. The summit is 150m to your left (bearing 120 degrees). Return to the gate and cross the hurdle next to it to keep the fence on your left as you descend W. Go through a gate at the col on to a path which joins the main Skiddaw route to bring you back to the fenced-in path and the carpark.

Walk 63   The bothy near Great Lingy Fell

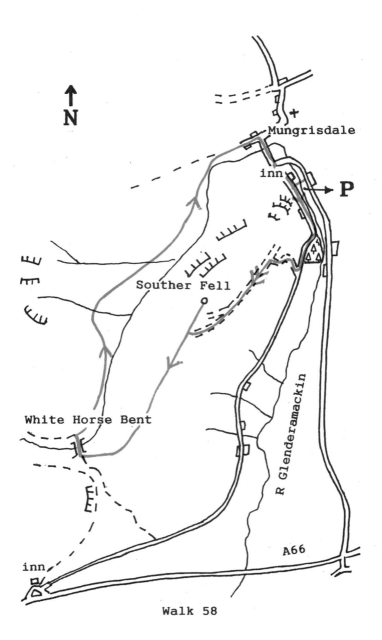

N

Mungrisdale

inn

P

Souther Fell

White Horse Bent

R Glenderamackin

A66

inn

Walk 58

58.   *Souther Fell*

Ordnance Survey map no: 90/OL 5/Pathfinder 576
Starting point: NY 364302
Walking distance: 8km/5ml
Amount of climbing: 300m/1,000ft

An attractive walk over a small fell which is unusual in being almost surrounded by one beck. Many witnesses testified that on Midsummer day 1745 an army marched all day across the fell. No trace of it was ever found, however.

Park opposite the green-painted village hall in Mungrisdale, off the A66. There is other parking near the end of the walk.

Cross the footbridge, go up to the inn and turn left. Pass through a gate across the road and just past the end of a small wood on the left a track starts on the right, curving round before going straight up to meet an indistinct track across the hillside. Turn left and after crossing a marshy patch a clear, straight path will be seen slanting up through the bracken. At the fork go left. When the path peters out climb to the ridge and turn right for the summit.

Retrace your steps and continue by following the ridge SW down to the col and then dropping down to the bridge on the right. Turn right and follow the river on your right to a lane through the village. Turn right for the carpark.

N

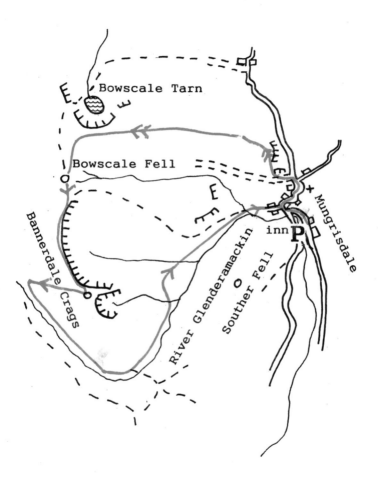

Bowscale Tarn

Bowscale Fell

Bannerdale Crags

River Glenderamackin

Souther Fell

inn **P**

Mungrisdale

Walk 59

59.   *Bowscale Fell and Bannerdale Crags*

Ordnance Survey map no: 90/OL 5/Pathfinder 576
Starting point: NY 364302
Walking distance: 13km/8ml
Amount of climbing: 530m/1,750ft

An open, airy walk on the fringe of the area with a good view
of Blencathra's Sharp Edge.

Park as for Walk 58.

Walk N on the road, pass the church and at the road
junction to Hutton Roof turn left behind a house where there
is a track. Go through the gate and at once climb steeply up
to the right past an old quarry to reach the ridge. Go W over
several false tops before turning SW to the shelter on
Bowscale Fell. Continue on a path going S but at a marshy
area work left to the path visible on the edge of the
escarpment. This leads to the summit of Bannerdale Crags.
To descend, go W to the col below Blencathra. Double back
to the left and you will be on a well-made path going SE with
the River Glenderamackin on your right. Follow the path
right down to the telephone box in the village. The carpark is
just to your right.

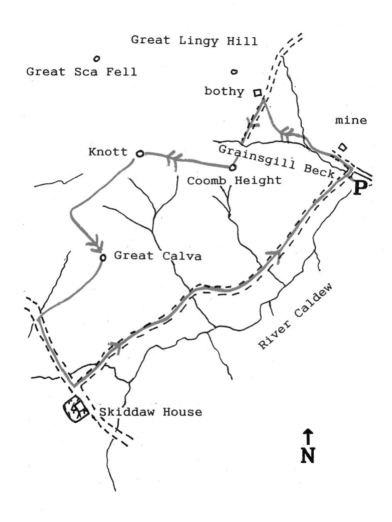

Great Lingy Hill

Great Sca Fell

bothy

mine

Knott

Grainsgill Beck

Coomb Height

P

Great Calva

River Caldew

Skiddaw House

N

Walk 60

60. *Knott and Great Calva*

Ordnance Survey map no: 90
Starting point: NY 327327
Walking distance: 15km/9ml
Amount of climbing: 650m/2,150ft

A walk over terrain more like the Pennines than the Lake
District, usually very quiet and demanding to navigate in
mist.

There is a rocky parking area at the end of a minor road
just across a bridge, and riverside parking a few hundred
metres downstream. Turn off the A66 at a sp to Mungrisdale.
Turn left by a phone box at a sp to Mosedale 2km/1.25ml N
of the village.

Go up a gated mine road sp PUBLIC BRIDLEWAY, continue
on the track through some old mine workings and then follow
a path by the beck. At a junction of becks go right to an easy
crossing place and with the beck on your right pass some
sheepfolds. An ill-defined path moves away from the beck
and leads to a bothy. Turn left. Beyond a beck a thin path
climbs to Coomb Height and turns right on the ridge on 288
degrees, petering out before the final pull up to Knott. From
the small cairn descend on 240 degrees to find a path to a col.
This becomes well defined as it rises to meet the remains of
an iron fence leading to the summit of Great Calva.

Continue on the little ridge to the cairns at the far end. The
path may not be easy to see at first but is approximately S and
leads to a stony track. Turn left to reach Skiddaw House
youth hostel. Turn left at the wall before the hostel on a track
going NE, cross a bridge and turn right on an improving track
leading to the carpark.

To shorten this walk retrace your steps from Knott and
descend the ridge from Coomb Height. Save 6.5km/4ml.

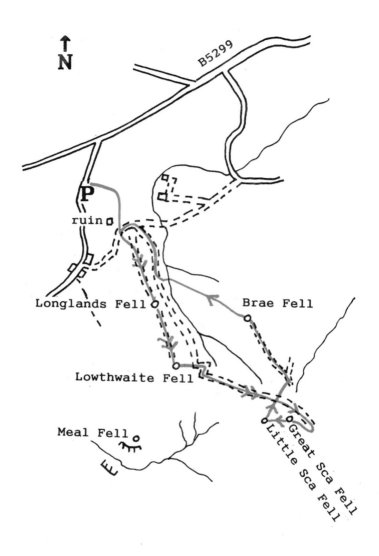

N

B5299

P

ruin

Longlands Fell

Brae Fell

Lowthwaite Fell

Meal Fell

Great Sca Fell

Little Sca Fell

Walk 61

61. *Great Sca Fell*

Ordnance Survey map no: 90
Starting point: NY 266369
Walking distance: 9.6km/6ml
Amount of climbing: 485m/1,600ft

A good walk to save for times when other fells are crowded. Mostly on unmapped green tracks and with views to Scotland as well as of the NW fells.

Park near a cattle-grid on a minor road NE of Uldale. Turn off the A591 NW of Keswick at a sp to Caldbeck by the Castle Inn.

A hundred metres N of the cattle-grid a green track goes E from the lane. Follow the wall on your right past a ruined farmhouse, maintaining direction to a broad track (old road). Cross and ascend the slopes opposite to the ridge where a clear track leads to the cairn on Longlands Fell and the minute cairn on Lowthwaite Fell. From this cairn follow a bearing of 90 degrees for a bend in the track at the far side of the col. Climb on this track which does not quite go to the summit of Great Sca Fell. When it levels out on a plateau go right. Great Sca Fell is the broad, unmarked area above. Cross it to the cairn and shelter on Little Sca Fell.

Descend on a bearing of 60 degrees, cross the track you have come up on and drop to another track which can be seen clearly leading to Brae Fell. Follow a bearing of 300 degrees down a broad ridge over rough, tussocky grass and look for the easiest place to cross the beck. Climb the bank and turn right on a track down to the old road. Turn left to join the outward route.

To shorten the walk, turn left on the track down the valley after descending from Lowthwaite Fell. Save 2km/1.25ml.

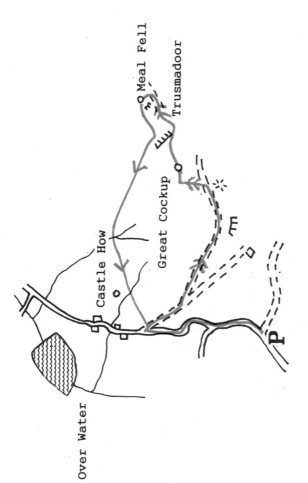

N

Meal Fell

Trusmadoor

Great Cockup

Castle How

Over Water

P

Walk 62

62. *Great Cockup and Meal Fell*

Ordnance Survey map no: 90
Starting point: NY 249323
Walking distance: 11km/7ml
Amount of climbing: 425m/1,400ft

A walk in a lovely area where paths and tracks are intermittent. By watching for main objectives ahead, though, it is
not too difficult to keep on the right line.

Park in a small carpark on the E side of a minor road sp to
Orthwaite off the A591 NW of Keswick.

Go NE on the lane for 1.6km and turn right at a bridleway
sp. Turn left on to a green path at the next sp and where the
path begins to level out by a low outcrop on the right, look
left for a small path leading up to a boulder on the skyline.
On the ridge turn right over trackless ground for the summit
of Great Cockup. Continue E towards a col (Trusmadoor),
curving right to avoid a low crag. Ascend the broad track
opposite. When the track levels out go up to the summit
shelter which can be glimpsed above to the left.

Follow the cairns SW back to Trusmadoor and turn right
on a track. When this peters out at a marsh by a knoll,
maintain height on a path across the hillside until the track is
met again. Turn left. The track traverses the hillside making
for a low col with a group of trees on a knoll to the right.
Beyond the first beck fork left and from the second beck by
some trees follow the line of a wall on your right back to the
bridleway. Turn right and then left on the lane for the carpark.

To shorten the walk omit Meal Fell. Save 3km/2ml.

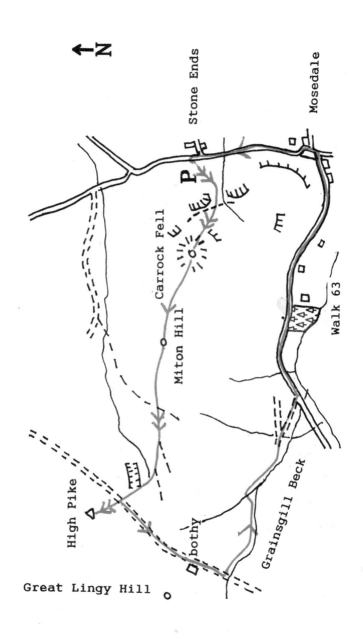

N

Stone Ends

Mosedale

P

Carrock Fell

Miton Hill

Walk 63

Grainsgill Beck

High Pike

bothy

Great Lingy Hill

63. Carrock Fell

Ordnance Survey map no: 90/Pathfinder 576
Starting point: NY 354337
Walking distance: 15km/9ml
Amount of climbing: 550m/1,820ft

Carrock Fell is better known to geologists and archaeologists than to most walkers. There is a massive hill-fort on the summit while the rocks are varied and full of anomalies, including Skye gabbro on the E side.

Take the minor road off the A66 sp to Mungrisdale and drive through the village. Fork left and pass the entrance to Mosedale. Two hundred metres past Stone Ends farm there is ample off-road parking on the left.

A grassy rake can be seen running up from right to left below the crags. Climb this and then go up and across a short patch of scree. Just before a beck go up a steep, green gully and at its head continue over a crossing track on to a path which is grassy at first. Cairns lead past a sheepfold to the summit. Continue W towards the little rise of Miton Hill on faint paths between boggy areas. The next immediate objective is a large cairn on the skyline and another beyond that, the path becoming more definite. A track is crossed after which the ground begins to rise again and two fainter paths to the left are passed. A hundred metres past the head of a gully a broad, stony track is met. Cross and continue to High Pike (with a shelter, TP, and memorial seat).

Return to the track and turn right to reach a bothy (always open). At the next beck turn left and descend with the beck on your right. The path is narrow and fitful but never goes far from the beck. At some mine workings take the right fork leading to the valley road. Follow it to a T-junction and turn left to reach the parking area, keeping to the grass verges most of the way.

To shorten this walk omit the ascent of High Pike. Save 1km/0.6ml.

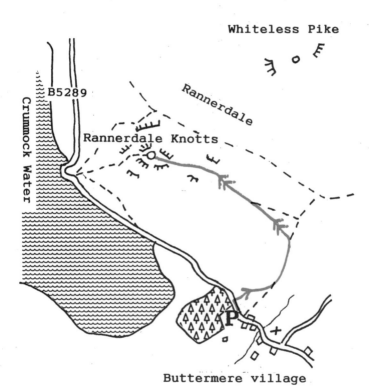

Whiteless Pike

Rannerdale

B5289

Crummock Water

Rannerdale Knotts

P

Buttermere village

Walk 64

THE NORTH-WESTERN FELLS

64. Rannerdale Knotts

Ordnance Survey map no: 89/OL 4
Starting point: NY 173172
Walking distance: 5km/3ml
Amount of climbing: 260m/850ft

An agreeable short walk to a good viewpoint. Rannerdale was the site of a battle in which the Normans were defeated in a late uprising.

Park in the NT carpark on the S side of the B5289 on the NW edge of Buttermere village. You will find other parking above the church and by the Fish hotel.

Walk 65   The summit of Castle Crag

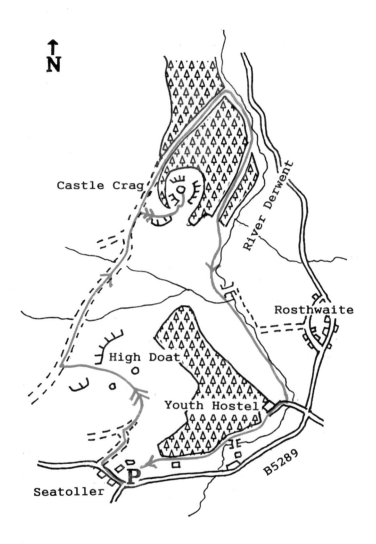

N

Castle Crag

River Derwent

Rosthwaite

High Doat

Youth Hostel

B5289

P

Seatoller

Walk 65

Turn left from the carpark, cross the road and after 50m turn right at a sp, following a wall on your left. After a boggy area the path curves left to join another path from the village. At a fork go left on to the ridge to the summit cairn. Return by the same route. (The path on the map down to the lake is cairned but not recommended.)

65. High Doat and Castle Crag

Ordnance Survey map no: 89 or 90/OL 4
Starting point: NY 246138
Walking distance: 9.6km/6ml
Amount of climbing: 210m/700ft

A walk through the Jaws of Borrowdale which has a special attraction in autumn. Wainwright thought it 'the loveliest square mile in Lakeland'.

Park in the NT carpark at Seatoller on the B5289 S of Keswick.

Return to the road and turn right. Go through a gate on the right between large square gateposts. After a second gate turn right, go through another gate after 50m and go uphill on a clear path to a gate in a wall. Fork left after a cairn in a pool to the twin summits of High Doat. Descend to a gate and to a ladder-stile on the far side on the valley. Turn right on the track.

The ascent of Castle Crag begins by a cairn at the top of a rise just past some wire sheep-pens. The path hugs the cliff on the right as far as a fence. Keep the fence on your right, crossing at the second stile and going over a ladder-stile nearby. Go up the path on the right to a zig-zag path over slate spoil and then to the war memorial on the summit. Retrace your steps to the track and turn right. At the river turn right at a sp to Rosthwaite. Shortly after passing through a wall take the fork on the left. Do not cross the stone bridge but continue on a narrow path with the river on your left. At the end of a permissive path turn right on the road which passes directly in front of the youth hostel, and then on to a track through the wood. Do not cross Folly Bridge on the left. The path leads into the carpark.

To shorten the walk, omit the ascent of Castle Crag. Save 0.4km/0.25ml.

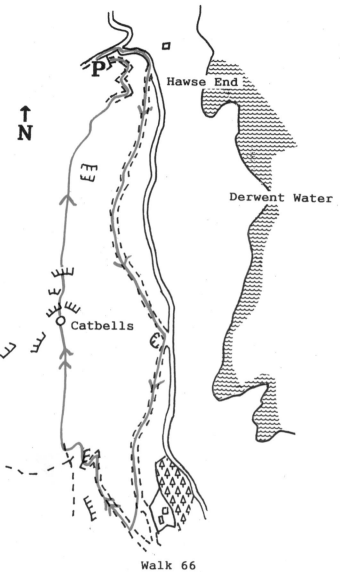

P

Hawse End

N

Derwent Water

Catbells

Walk 66

66. Catbells

Ordnance Survey map no: 89 or 90/OL 4
Starting point: NY 246211
Walking distance: 6km/3.75ml
Amount of climbing: 400m/1,350ft

A deservedly popular peak with enchanting views in all directions. To avoid crowds try a sunrise or sunset ascent.

Park in a carpark off a minor road near Hawse End S of Keswick. You will find other off-road parking in both directions nearby or by the village hall in Stair, 1km/0.6ml to the W.

From the carpark turn right and after 200m turn right at a fork in the road. Turn right at a sp on to a bridleway which joins the road again briefly by a quarry before rising. Continue past a plaque to Sir Hugh Walpole and when the track reaches a wall take the right fork uphill. Turn right on a large track which leads over slabs to the col of Hause Gate. Turn right on a broad track over the summit and down the ridge to the carpark. Some rocks on the descent need careful negotiation.

Walk 66   Catbells

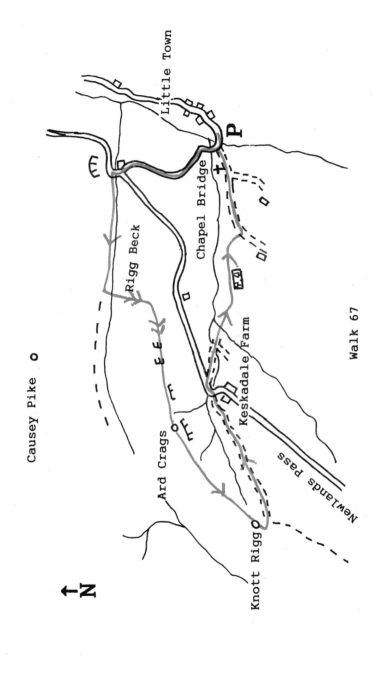

Causey Pike

Little Town

Rigg Beck

Chapel Bridge

P

Ard Crags

Keskadale Farm

Knott Rigg

Newlands Pass

Walk 67

N

67. Ard Crags and Knott Rigg

Ordnance Survey map no: 89/90/OL 4
Starting point: NY 232194
Walking distance: 9km/5.5ml
Amount of climbing: 450m/1,500ft

This is a short walk of high quality with excellent views from a good ridge.

Park in a small carpark E of Chapel Bridge on a minor road at Little Town, S of Keswick.

Turn left from the carpark. At a road junction turn right, cross the bridge and at once turn left up a small valley. Ford the beck when the wall beyond it goes uphill and climb to the crest of the ridge. Turn right and follow a steeply rising path which leads to Ard Crags and by a ridge to the cairn on Knott Rigg 2km beyond. Turn left, going E for a short way past a fenced-off boghole to the ridge which is followed down. Alternatively, just before the first rocky rise drop about 20m to the right to pick up an old drove road. Both routes meet by a fence where you turn left to reach the road.

Turn left and just across the bridge go through a sp gate on the right. Go through a gate ahead and over a bridge to the right. Turn left, cross another bridge and follow a track rising to the left. This ends at a field. Cross to an oak, left of which are a stile and bridge. Now follow the fence on your right over stiles and bridges with some marker posts. After crossing the fence on your right by a stile, further posts lead to stiles and a lane. Turn left, pass the church and reach the road where the carpark is just to your right.

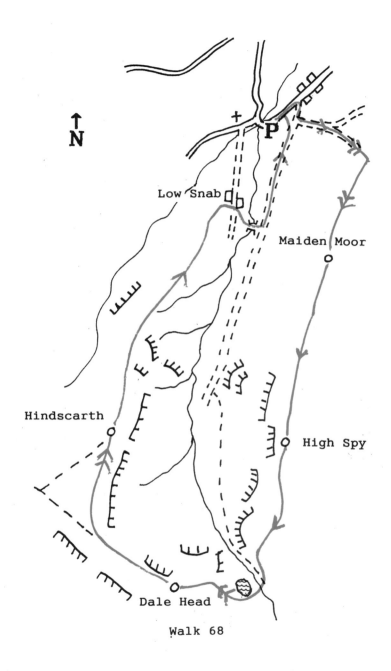

N

Low Snab

Maiden Moor

Hindscarth

High Spy

Dale Head

Walk 68

68. *High Spy to Hindscarth*

Ordnance Survey map no: 90/OL 4
Starting point: NY 232194
Walking distance: 14.5km/9ml
Amount of climbing: 820m/2,700ft

One of the fine ridge walks in this area giving sustained high-level walking on good terrain.

Park as for Walk 67.

Walk E from the carpark and turn right at a sp to Catbells and Manesty. Fork right on a mine road leading up to a cairned route and a col overlooking Derwent Water. Turn right on a clear path over Maiden Moor to the tall cairn with a seat on High Spy. The track drops to a tarn and sheepfold before climbing as a well-constructed path to the cairn on Dale Head. Continue NW and fork right to the shelter/cairn on Hindscarth. A clear track follows the ridge down to a wall. Turn right, pass the entrance to Low Snab farm on the left (refreshments) and then branch left to a footbridge. Turn left on a mine track and when the lane comes into view, take a short cut left to a stile and turn left for the carpark.

To shorten this walk turn right at a cairn before crossing the beck by the tarn and sheepfold below Dale Head. The track leads to Low Snab farm. (Details on Walk 70.) Save 1.5km/1ml.

Walk 69   Ascending Robinson

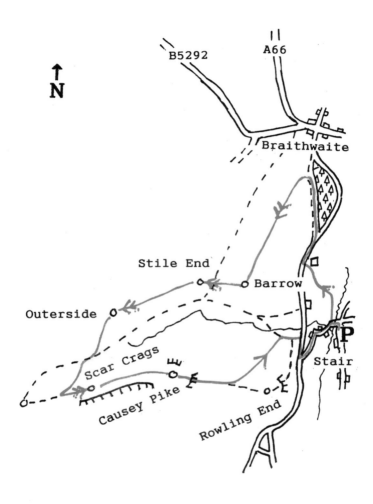

Walk 69

69. Causey Pike

Ordnance Survey map no: 89/OL 4
Starting point: NY 237212
Walking distance: 11km/6.5ml
Amount of climbing: 865m/2,855ft

The height gain makes this a testing short walk. Five, or optionally six, peaks with a fine ridge to finish provide an excellent route for a first visit to the Derwent Fells.

Park outside the village hall in Stair, near the telephone box (donation to hall funds) on a minor road S of Keswick. There is other roadside parking near Uzzicar farm.

From the carpark turn right and then left at road junction sp to Buttermere. Cross the bridge and turn right at a sp to Braithwaite. After 100m turn left at a sp and, with the hedge on your left, reach a stile. Keep the fence on your left until you see a gate half-right. Cross the stile next to it and go half-left to reach a lane. Turn right. Go left on a bridleway leading above a wood and near the far end turn left to the ridge leading to the summit of Barrow. Drop to a col (forks in the track rejoin), cross the main track and ascend Stile End. Outside is at 240 degrees, the path dropping to a col and curving to the right around a tarn before climbing.

From Outerside the objective is the col at 220 degrees. After a steep initial descent, the path crosses a bog to the left to the main track. Turn right up to the col on a good path hugging the base of the rocks on the left. Turn left at the col and follow the ridge over Scar Crags and Causey Pike. The descent is straight on over rock and down a small chimney, requiring extreme caution, especially if wet. At a col take the left fork for an easy descent to the lane by the bridge.

Alternatively, to complete the circuit take the right fork over Rowling End but be warned that the descent is steep and treacherous. In both cases turn right on the lane and double back on a hairpin bend sp to Stair to reach the carpark.

To shorten the walk turn left on the lane at Uzzicar farm and turn right up the track below Barrow. This leads to the col below Scar Crags. Save 2.5km/1.5ml.

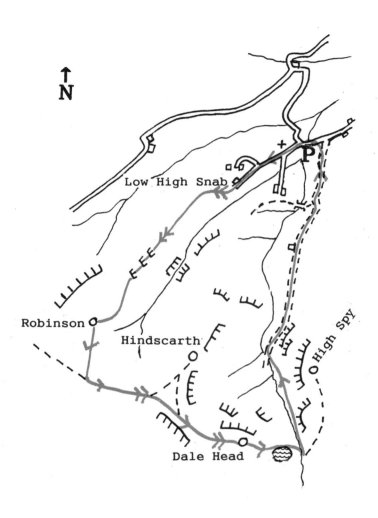

N

Low High Snab

P

Robinson

Hindscarth

High Spy

Dale Head

Walk 70

70. *Robinson and Dale Head*

Ordnance Survey map no: 90/OL 4
Starting point: NY 232194
Walking distance: 14.5km/9ml
Amount of climbing: 820m/2,700ft

Of the three ridges rising from Little Town, the one leading to Robinson is probably the finest to ascend. The return route is by the upper Newlands valley among magnificent rock scenery.

Park as for Walk 67.

Turn left from the carpark and just over the bridge turn left through a gate at a sp to Newlands church. Fork right at the church on a surfaced lane, pass the gateway to High Snab farm and go through a gate on a permissive path past Low High Snab. At a wall corner turn right up a steep bank to a post on the skyline. Turn left on the ridge path, crossing three rock steps before a broad plateau is reached. Cairns lead to the right over several false summits before the true summit is reached. Go S for 300m to reach a fence. Turn left and follow the fence to the first col and then a line of old fence posts to a second col and Dale Head.

Continue down a well-constructed path to a tarn and sheepfold. Cross the beck and follow it for a short distance until a cairn on the left indicates a path leaving the main track. Continue by the beck down to a green patch and then follow a cairned route through a small boulder-field. A high-level path traverses the fellside before descending gently to the mine road in the valley. When the lane is in sight take a short cut on the left to a stile and turn left for the carpark.

N

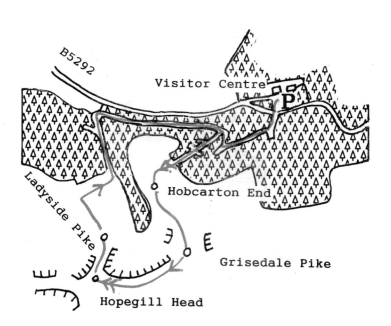

B5292

Visitor Centre

P

Hobcarton End

Ladyside Pike

Grisedale Pike

Hopegill Head

Walk 71

71. Grisedale Pike

Ordnance Survey map no: 89/OL 4
Starting point: NY 208245
Walking distance: 10km/6ml
Amount of climbing: 550m/1,800ft

The approach to this superb horseshoe ridge has been simplified by the Forestry Commission's newish numbered posts (referred to in the text). Not too difficult in mist.

Park at the visitor centre, Whinlatter Pass, on the B5292, W of Keswick.

Descend to the road on a sp path, turn left and cross to a surfaced road into the forest. Fork right (sp 43) and double back at the first junction on the right (arrow and sp 41). Turn left up a firebreak after 50m, fork left at orienteering post 78N and go over a crossing track. The path leads through the forest on to a ridge to the summit of Grisedale Pike, crossing one fence. (There is no path beyond the fence; follow a bearing of 160 degrees.)

Turn right at the summit slabs, follow the low wall to its end and then climb to Hopegill Head with cliffs on the right. The descent begins on a bearing of 50 degrees on a small path to the left of the ridge. Outward sloping slabs are potentially dangerous if wet and are best descended by a fault in the rock, keeping well away from the crags on your right. Follow the ridge/wall to Ladyside Pike and then as far as a junction of the wall and a fence. Turn right and follow the fence down steep, grassy slopes into the valley. Cross a gate near the bottom and make for a sheepfold and a footpath leading to a forest track. Fork right (sp 37), cross the bridge and go left at sp 36. Keep on this track for 1.5km to the outward route by sp 41, passing turnings on the right (sp 35), left (sp 32), and right (sp 33).

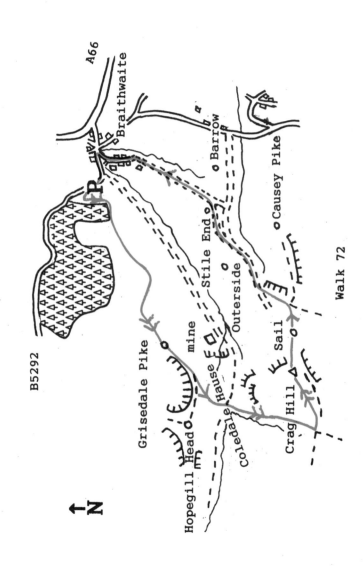

N

A66

Braithwaite

B5292

P

Barrow

Causey Pike

Stile End

Outerside

Walk 72

Grisedale Pike

mine

Sail

Hause

Crag Hill

Hopegill Head

Coledale

72. A Coledale Round

Ordnance Survey map no: 90/OL 4
Starting point: NY 227237
Walking distance: 15km/9.5ml
Amount of climbing: 1,060m/3,500ft

One of the classic Lake District rounds, a high-level ridge walk with a return on well-made mine paths.

Park on the S side of the B5292, Whinlatter Pass road, 400m W of Braithwaite off the A66 W of Keswick.

A sp at the N end of the carpark indicates the route to Grisedale Pike. Cross the stile and turn right up an increasingly rocky ridge to the summit, 3km away. Continue by following the old wall down and then over a subsidiary peak. Just over the summit take a fork left at a cairn to reach Coledale Hause. Ascend by the stream opposite up a grassy valley roughly S to reach a grassy plateau. Turn left at a crossing of tracks and after 100m fork left on a path to the TP on Crag Hill.

For the narrow ridge to Sail aim for a cairn at 120 degrees. The path continues over the summit to a col. Turn left on a path hugging the base of broken cliffs and dropping to a broad mine track. Note here three low hills on the left. Just as you have passed the first of these, fork left by a large cairn before the track drops and curves right. This path traverses below the second hill and then turns left to pass between the second and third. A broad green path develops and drops down to join an old road by a ruined farm. Turn left and join a tarmac lane below a gate. Fork right at the inn in Braithwaite, pass the Methodist church, cross the bridge to the B5292 and turn left for the carpark.

To shorten the walk, turn left at Coledale Hause on the mine road to Braithwaite. Save 2.5km/1.5ml.

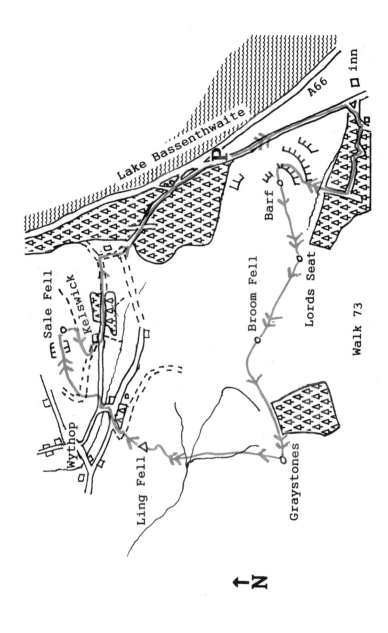

Lake Bassenthwaite

A66

inn

P

Sale Fell

Kelswick

Wythop

Ling Fell

Barf

Broom Fell

Lords Seat

Graystones

Walk 73

←N

73.   Lorton Fells

Ordnance Survey map no: 89/OL 4
Starting point: NY 218276
Walking distance: 16km/10ml
Amount of climbing: 985m/3,250ft

The six summits on this walk are all on easy terrain but provide a demanding day out in a green and tranquil area.

Woodend carpark is on the W side of the A66 at a junction with a minor road NW of Keswick.

Turn left along the lane and right at a sp for Lords Seat/Barf, opposite Powter How carpark. Turn right at the junction and at a left bend, cross a stile on the right on to a well sp path through the wood. Scramble up one crag and turn right at a forest road before leaving the plantation. Cross the beck and at a T-junction turn right for Barf. For Lords Seat follow a bearing of 290 degrees initially, the path curving to the left and over boggy ground to the summit with remains of an old fence. The path on a connecting grassy ridge to the 2m cairn on Broom Fell is at 310 degrees. Continue to Graystones on 290 degrees. Beyond a col, the path curves left, below the highest ground, then peters out. Maintain direction to the corner of a plantation and continue to its end before crossing a wooden fence on the left. Follow the fence/wall uphill to a bend, then continue to the summit a few metres beyond a crumbling wall. With this wall on your right, descend N, crossing it when a fence joins from the left. Cross the beck and keep near it for the driest ground. Cross two more becks and climb by a wall. Branch right when the wall bends left – no path – over steep, grassy slopes to the TP on Ling Fell. Descend on 30 degrees to a lane. Turn right, then left at a junction and right after crossing a bridge. Go through a gate and uphill by a wall. Turn left on a green track but leave it at the top of the rise to turn right on a broad, grassy path to the neat cairn on Sale Fell just past some rock outcrops.

Descend S and after a few metres a Y-junction of old walls will be seen. Turn right on a track above them and at the next track junction turn left down to Kelswick farm. Turn left on the lane, pass a sp on the right and cross a stile by a gate ahead

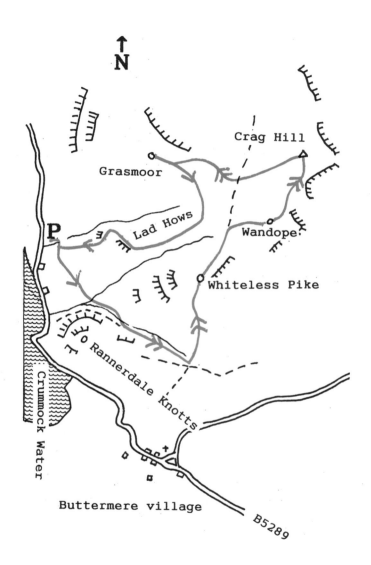

N

Crag Hill

Grasmoor

Lad Hows

P

Wandope

Whiteless Pike

Rannerdale Knotts

Crummock Water

Buttermere village

B5289

Walk 74

on to a green lane leading into a wood. Pass the site of Wythop Old Church. Go left at a fork. After leaving the wood go through a gate on the right at the end of a short stretch of wall. Pass a pond on the left and turn left at the next track joined. Enter a wood, cross a forestry road and descend to a lane. Turn right and go through a bus turning circle on to a disused road back to the carpark.

To shorten this walk, go E from the summit of Lords Seat and follow the fence to a stile into the wood. Save 9.5km/6ml.

74. *Whiteless Pike to Grasmoor*

Ordnance Survey map no: 89/OL 4
Starting point: NY 162194
Walking distance: 12km/7.5ml
Amount of climbing: 940m/3,100ft

This range is characterised by high, green hills supported by broken crags and scree, making for hard ascents and difficult navigation on top if conditions are poor.

Park on the W side of the B5289, NW of Buttermere just past Rannerdale farm. There is another carpark 100m N and several other roadside spaces nearby.

Take the track going out of the back of the carpark, cross the beck and follow a path over the footbridge on the right to reach a small col just past a sheepfold. Turn left on the track which zig-zags uphill to Whiteless Pike. Continue on the ridge and at a cairn take a bearing of 70 degrees over grass to Wandope. Follow the rim of the escarpment (340 degrees initially) and when near a line of cairns on your left move to them and follow them to the summit of Crag Hill. Retrace your steps to the col and ascend Grasmoor.

To descend, reverse the route for 200m. Just past a large cairn a line of smaller cairns indicates the route down to the grassy ridge of Lad Hows. Bear right at the end of the ridge and then turn left on a track following the beck to the carpark.

This walk may be shortened by omitting the ascents of Wandope and Crag Hill. Continue direct to the col from Whiteless Pike and turn left for Grasmoor. Save 1.6km/1ml.

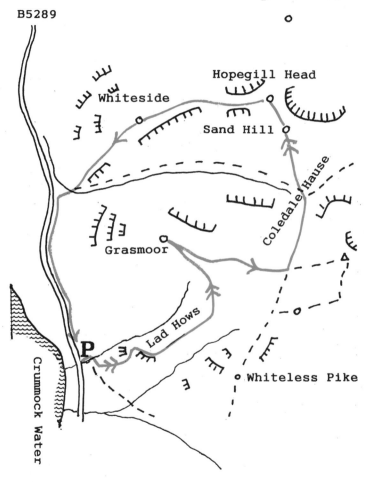

N

B5289

Ladyside Pike

Hopegill Head

Whiteside

Sand Hill

Coledale Hause

Grasmoor

Lad Hows

Crummock Water

Whiteless Pike

Walk 75

75. *Grasmoor to Whiteside*

Ordnance Survey map no: 89/OL 4
Starting point: NY 162194
Walking distance: 12km/7.5ml
Amount of climbing: 970m/3,200ft

A good high-level walk over difficult ground with a fine ridge near the end.

Park as for Walk 74.

Take the track going from the back of the carpark, cross the beck and immediately turn left going uphill with the beck on your left. The track gradually becomes more defined and turns to the right over a crag and then left on a grassy ridge leading to shelters on the summit of Grasmoor.

Retrace your steps, passing the point of ascent, and continue on a track round the head of the valley, over a subsidiary peak and down to a col. Turn left through a little valley to Coledale Hause, taking a left fork just above the lowest point. Take the path opposite going N uphill to Hopegill Head. Turn left and follow the ridge to Whiteside, then maintain direction downhill over broken rock and scree with crags on the left.

Cross a footbridge to reach the road and turn left for the carpark, using grassy verges.

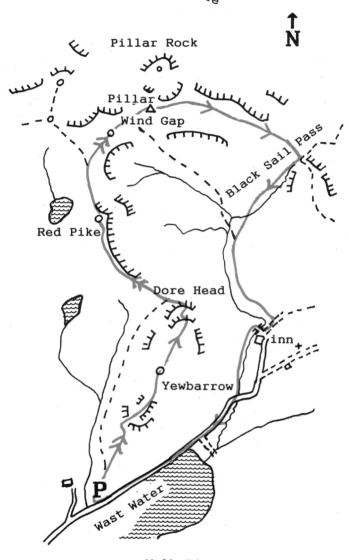

Ennerdale

N

Pillar Rock

Pillar
Wind Gap

Black Sail Pass

Red Pike

Dore Head

inn

Yewbarrow

P

Wast Water

Walk 76

THE WESTERN FELLS

76. *Pillar*

Ordnance Survey map no: 89/OL 4
Starting point: NY 168068
Walking distance: 15km/9ml
Amount of climbing: 1,140m/3,750ft

One consolation on this route is that after the first ascent, which is steep, the height gain on each successive summit is less and the gradient easier. Some scrambling on Yewbarrow.

Park in the NT carpark on the N side of Wastwater Road just by Overbeck Bridge.

Leave by the footpath at the back of the carpark with the beck on your left. Cross a ladder-stile and ascend to a steep scree gully. At a cleft in the rock (Great Door) turn left for the summit of Yewbarrow and then follow cairns over the ridge to steep rocks down to Dore Head. Follow the path opposite up to Red Pike. Descend and follow a path curving to the right round the head of the valley. Ascend Black Crag and drop to Wind Gap before climbing to the TP on Pillar.

Descend on a well-worn path following a line of old fence posts to Black Sail Pass overlooked by the crags of Kirk Fell ahead. Turn right on a loose, stony track leading down to the back of the Wasdale Head hotel. (Work on repairing this footpath is to begin in 1994.) Cross the pack-horse bridge on the right and follow the beck downstream to the road. Continue to the carpark.

It is possible to shorten this walk by descending from Wind Gap. Save 2.5km/1.5ml.

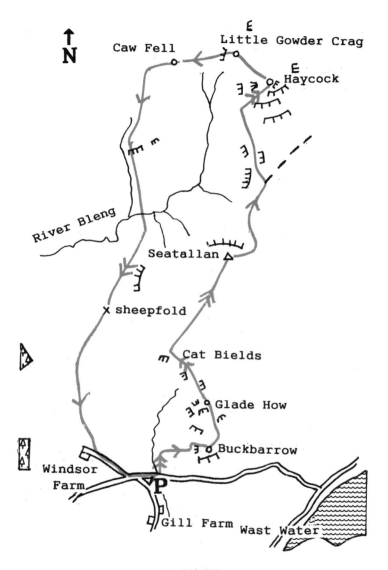

N

Caw Fell

E
Little Gowder Crag

E
Haycock

River Bleng

Seatallan

x sheepfold

Cat Bields

Glade How

Buckbarrow

Windsor
Farm

P

Gill Farm   Wast Water

Walk 77

77.   *Buckbarrow to Caw Fell*

Ordnance Survey map no: 89/OL 6
Starting point: NY 129054
Walking distance: 18.5km/11.5ml
Amount of climbing: 1,075m/3,550ft

Although this walk is almost entirely on grass it is exacting
because there are few paths. It is a part of Wasdale that most
walkers ignore but which can be recommended.

Adequate parking can be found by the entrance to Gill
farm on the Gosforth to Wasdale Head road.

About 10m E of the carpark climb the path following Gill
Beck on the N side of the road. A distinct path reaches a small
outcrop where the ground levels out. Turn right and, keeping
to the edge of the escarpment, make for the crags of
Buckbarrow. A path will be found which goes to their left and
to the cairn on the edge of the crag. Keep E for the next cairn
and then N to the cairn on Glade How. Follow a bearing of
350 degrees over a series of rocky knolls, one with a large
cairn, to the cairn on the skyline which is above Cat Bields.
From here long, grassy slopes lead NE to the TP on Seatallan.
Ahead is a rocky descent avoided by turning right to grassy
slopes to the track visible below. Also note from here a grassy
rake to the left of Haycock which is your way up. Just past a
rusty iron pen take the left fork in the path. When this peters
out keep near the rocky outcrops ahead, making always for
the grassy rake at the foot of which is a cairn. A steep climb
now brings you to the summit of Haycock which is by a wall.
For Caw Fell follow the wall NW over Little Gowder Crag.
The pink cairn is on the N side of the wall.

Start the descent by following the wall to where it makes
a sharp turn to the right. Here go S. You will reach marshy
patches which soon become a beck in a deepening gorge.
Keep this beck on your right and when a rocky area is
reached stay close to the beck, picking your way through the
rocks with care but without real difficulty. A few cairns guide
you down to the River Bleng which must be forded. Choose
not only a shallow spot but one which avoids bogs. On the
far side you will find only sheep-tracks but turn right on them
as they stay above the marshes. Short sections of the

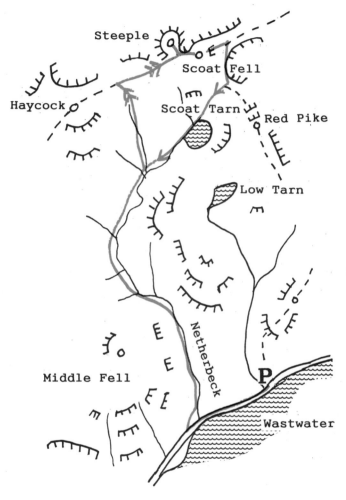

N

Steeple

Scoat Fell

Haycock

Scoat Tarn

Red Pike

Low Tarn

Middle Fell

Netherbeck

P

Wastwater

Walk 78

bridleway appear, one where rocks have been cleared through a boulder-field, and gradually the path rises to the left, leaving the river to cross a shoulder of land. From a circular sheepfold vehicle-tracks define the way and lead to more folds by a wall which is followed down to the access road to Windsor farm. Turn left to reach the road and left again for the carpark.

78.   *Scoat Fell and Steeple*

Ordnance Survey map no: 89/OL 4
Starting point: NY 168068
Walking distance: 16km/10ml
Amount of climbing: 775m/2,550ft

The stony valley path makes this walk more difficult than might appear. It is memorable, however, for the arête to Steeple and for Scoat Tarn, Wainwright's 'gem in a wild setting'.

Park as for Walk 76.

Turn right on the road and after 2km turn right at a sp on a green path which joins the W bank of Nether Beck. Follow the beck for 5km to a col where there is a wall, and turn right. On level ground a large cairn indicates the route left to Steeple which is a few minutes away to the N but over a narrow arête. Return to the cairn and to the summit of Scoat Fell, marked by a cairn on the wall itself.

Follow the wall a little further and go through a gap and over boulders to reach a path again. Shortly after, double back on a path joining from the right. This traverses the fellside and leads to a col. At a cairn descend on a bearing of 210 degrees and a path develops which leads down past Scoat Tarn and to the valley. Cross the becks by the sheepfolds to the far side of the valley and turn left on your outward route.

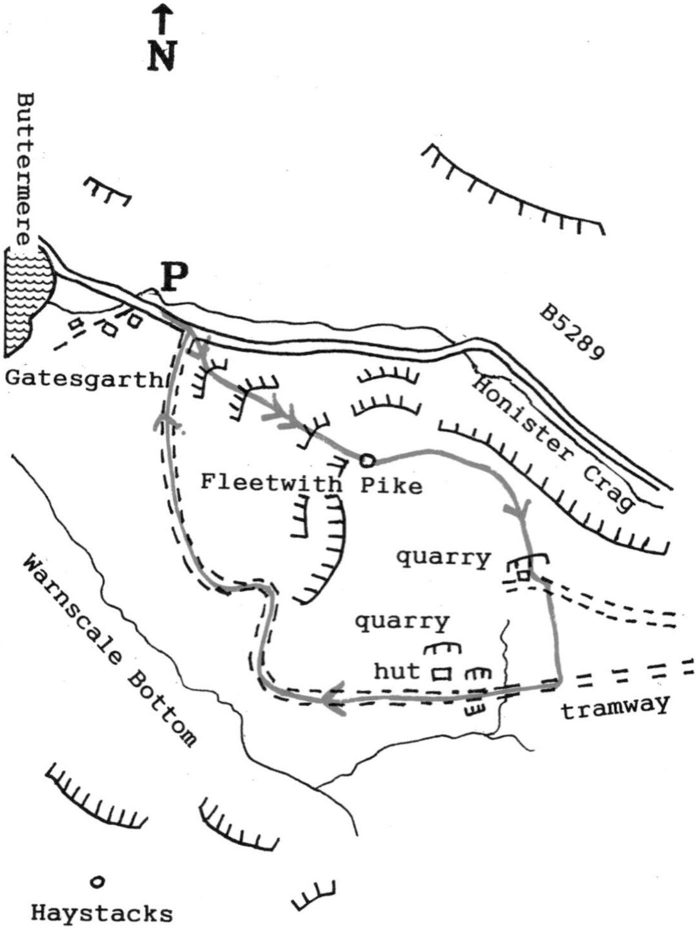

N

Buttermere

P

Gatesgarth

B5289

Honister Crag

Fleetwith Pike

quarry

quarry

hut

tramway

Warnscale Bottom

Haystacks

Walk 79

Walk 79   Haystacks and Pillar

79.   Fleetwith Pike

Ordnance Survey map no: 89/OL 4
Starting point: NY 195149
Walking distance: 6.5km/4ml
Amount of climbing: 530m/1,750ft

The very steep ascent of Fleetwith Pike is made easier by being in several steps, giving the chance for an occasional rest. Warnscale Bottom, the return route, is a huge rock amphitheatre with waterfalls.

There is a carpark (fee) at Gatesgarth farm on the B5289, SE of Buttermere and free parking for a few early arrivals 400m further E.

Turn left from the carpark and turn right at a sp after 100m. Go across the grass towards the white cross on the rocks, not along the stony track. A good path with some easy scrambling leads direct to the summit. Maintain direction with the crags on your left until the path swings right just past the second tarn. The path enters an old quarry. Turn left by a rusty tin hut and soon take a green path to the right leading to an old tramway. Turn right and follow this down, through another quarry and past the ruins of a climbing hut. A good track follows the right-hand side of the valley back to the carpark.

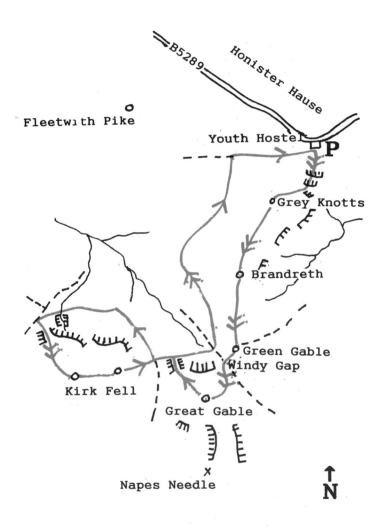

B5289

Honister Hause

Fleetwith Pike

Youth Hostel

P

Grey Knotts

Brandreth

Green Gable

Windy Gap

Kirk Fell

Great Gable

Napes Needle

N

Walk 80

80.   Great Gable

Ordnance Survey map no: 89/OL 4
Starting point: NY 225135
Walking distance: 16km/10ml
Amount of climbing: 1,100m/3,600ft

A strenuous walk to one of Lakeland's most popular peaks. The return is by a high-level traverse reputedly used by one Moses Rigg to transport the poteen he distilled in a hut high on Gable Crag.

Park in the NT carpark at the rear of the youth hostel on Honister Hause, on the S side of the B5289.

Follow the sp to Grey Knotts (the sp to Great Gable indicates the return route). The route zig-zags up a well-constructed path on the line of a fence. Follow the fence to the second stile and cross to go up right to the summit of Grey Knotts. Follow a line of old iron fence posts past a tarn to Brandreth and follow a further line of posts going S to reach a col with tarns below Green Gable. A well-worn and cairned route leads over Green Gable, down to Windy Gap and up to Great Gable with some scrambling.

From the summit go NW to pick up a line of cairns going down steep rock and scree to a col below Kirk Fell. Turn right by a large cairn on a flat rock on to a small path winding around the mountainside. This crosses a beck below a gorge and climbs up to Black Sail Pass. Turn left and follow a path round the base of the crags. When scree is reached, move right on to a worn route on a rocky rib, again roughly on a line of old fence posts. After a last tricky little chimney go over easier ground, following fence posts to the summit of Kirk Fell.

The descent is again by fence posts over a subsidiary summit with a good view of Napes Needle at the base of the ridge on the right flank of Gable. A cairned path leads down to the col below Gable. Follow fence posts over a rocky rib and continue on a clear path on the fellside opposite – Moses' Trod. Below Brandreth a track joins from the right with many cairns. Follow a cairned path heading for the slate quarries. The track turns right at a wall and follows the tramway down to the carpark.

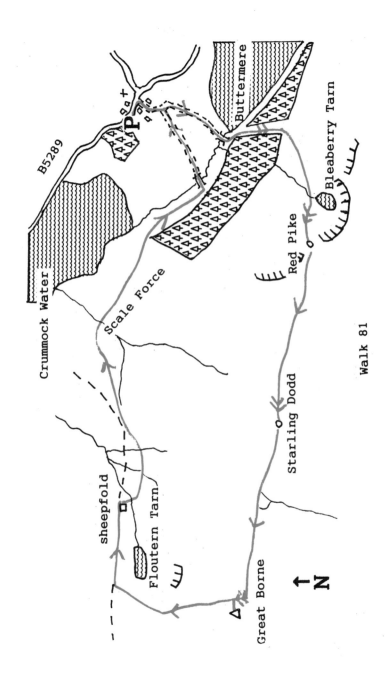

B5289

Crummock Water

Buttermere

Bleaberry Tarn

Red Pike

Scale Force

sheepfold

Floutern Tarn

Starling Dodd

Great Borne

Walk 81

N

To shorten this walk omit the ascent of Kirk Fell, turning right on to Moses' Trod at the foot of Gable. Save 3km/2ml and 180m/600ft.

81.   Red Pike to Great Borne

Ordnance Survey map no: 89/OL 4
Starting point: NY 173172
Walking distance: 14.5km/9ml
Amount of climbing: 880m/2,900ft

An unfrequented area, apart from Red Pike. Navigation is difficult in mist, paths being faint and discontinuous. There is one difficult marshy area on the descent.

Park as for Walk 64.

Turn right from the carpark and right again by the Bridge hotel. Take the sp path going to the left of the Fish hotel, cross the bridge and turn right at a sp to Red Pike. Climb a well-made path through the wood, emerging into the combe near Bleaberry Tarn. A path on the right ascends the NE ridge to the summit of Red Pike.

Descend steeply W over scree and rock to a grassy plateau and cross a line of fence posts on a green path going NW initially. After crossing a further line of posts the path is at times indistinct with an occasional cairn to the grassy summit of Starling Dodd. Maintain direction and at a col follow a broad green track towards Great Borne. The track joins a fence which takes a sharp turn to the right. At the top of a rise turn left for the TP and shelter on the summit. Return to the fence, turn left and follow the fence down steep ground to the valley. Cross a stile on the right, negotiate a swamp and go up to a faint green path by a gate. Turn right.

At a sp for mountain bikes fork right, following the fence to a gate. Go half-right to a sheepfold. From this point ignore stiles and the mapped route which goes through a dangerous swamp. Go right to firmer ground slightly above the valley bottom and then left to a line of cairns. The path emerges from the boggy area and is intermittent until it rises and curves right when Buttermere comes into view. Cross the bridge below Scale Force.

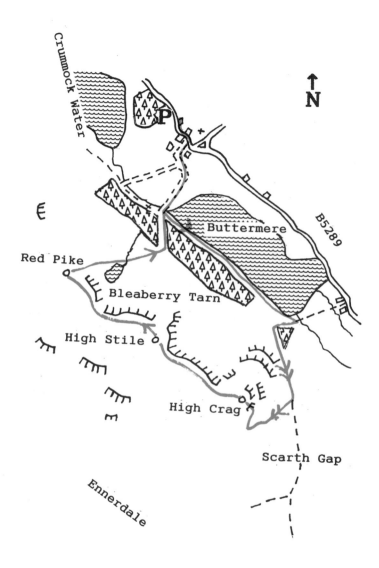

N

Crummock Water

P

+

B5289

Buttermere

Red Pike

Bleaberry Tarn

High Stile

High Crag

Scarth Gap

Ennerdale

Walk 82

A very rough and stony route now leads down to the lake. Turn through a gate on your left, cross a bridge and follow the track to the Fish hotel.

82. *Scarth Gap to Red Pike*

Ordnance Survey map no: 89/OL 4
Starting point: NY 173172
Walking distance: 11km/7ml
Amount of climbing: 790m/2,600ft

A strenuous walk over rocky ground with good views of Ennerdale and Pillar Rock.

Park as for Walk 64.

Turn right from the carpark and right again by the Bridge hotel. Take a sp path going to the left of the Fish hotel. Pass sp to Scale Force and to Red Pike. Keep on the lakeside path to the end of the lake and turn right at a sp to ENNERDALE VIA SCARTH GAP. The path rises above a plantation and across the fellside. At a wall turn right and follow the path to the col below High Crag. To avoid a scree slope look for the path which traverses left and then climbs on grass before traversing right on to a track in loose rock. From High Crag take a path following a line of old fence posts NW, finally curving right to the summit of High Stile. Keep NW for Red Pike on the ridge with crags on the right.

Walk 83   Haystacks

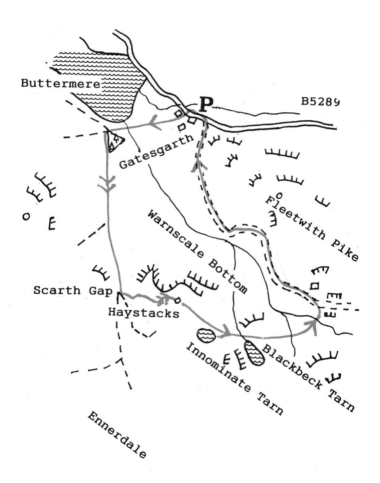

N

Buttermere

P   B5289

Gatesgarth

Fleetwith Pike

Warnscale Bottom

Scarth Gap

Haystacks

Innominate Tarn

Blackbeck Tarn

Ennerdale

Walk 83

Walk 83   The summit of Haystacks

To descend, go directly down the NE ridge to Bleaberry Tarn and follow a well-made track through the wood, over a bridge and back to the Fish hotel.

83.   Haystacks

Ordnance Survey map no: 89/OL 4
Starting point: NY 195149
Walking distance: 8km/5ml
Amount of climbing: 485m/1,600ft

'. . . For beauty, variety and interesting detail, for sheer fascination and unique individuality, the summit area of Haystacks is supreme.' So wrote A.Wainwright whose ashes are scattered here. Climb it and judge for yourself.
 Park as for Walk 79.
 Cross the road and go through the gate by the sheep pens sp LAKESIDE PATH. The track crosses a footbridge and rises by a plantation to Scarth Gap. Turn left by some iron fence posts and after 50m take the left fork on a path which negotiates a series of small crags. The summit is on a rocky tor immediately behind a small tarn.
 To descend, continue SE on a well-worn track, passing two tarns on your right. The track swings left, dropping to a beck

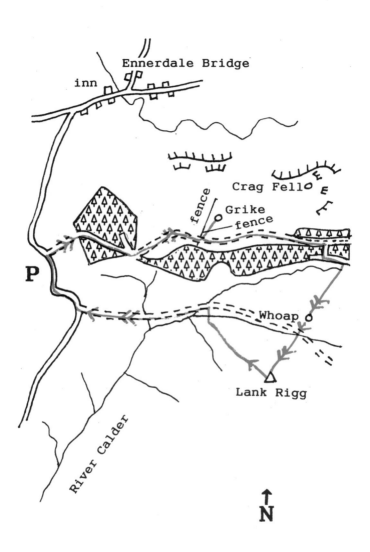

Ennerdale Bridge

inn

Crag Fell

fence

Grike

fence

P

Whoap

Lank Rigg

River Calder

N

Walk 84

with an old quarry on the far side. Cross and turn left on a broad track leading down to the carpark.

84. Grike and Lank Rigg

Ordnance Survey map no: 89/OL 4
Starting point: NY 061136
Walking distance: 12km/7.5ml
Amount of climbing: 485m/1,600ft

A quiet place to walk and explore. Just N of the starting point and on the E side of the road is a restored stone circle.

The grid reference is for the sp at the start of the walk. There are numerous parking places off the fell road which is just S of Ennerdale Bridge, E of Cleator Moor (on the A5086).

Follow the old mine road sp PUBLIC BRIDLEWAY RED BECK. The track passes through a plantation. Ignore turnings to the left and right and curve left with the wood now on the right only. At the top of a rise turn left at a fence and cross the fence in front. Climb at an angle between fences to reach three cairns on the summit of Grike in 200m. Return to the track and continue, re-entering the forest. Twenty metres beyond the cairn on the left turn down a firebreak on the right. Turn left at a junction and cross a stile on your right. Take a bearing of 210 degrees for the grassy summit of Whoap – no paths and many marshes.

From the flat, grassy summit keep on the same bearing until the col below Lank Rigg is visible. From here a small, defined path leads directly to the TP on the summit. A cairn 200m further on is a good viewpoint and lunch spot. Descend on a bearing of 335 degrees from the TP and cross the beck near a circular sheepfold, continuing to the track beyond. Turn left and ford the beck. Immediately beyond the next beck the track swings away to the right up a side valley. There are several forks in the track but the right of way is the left-hand track. Drop down to the fell road and turn right to reach the starting point.

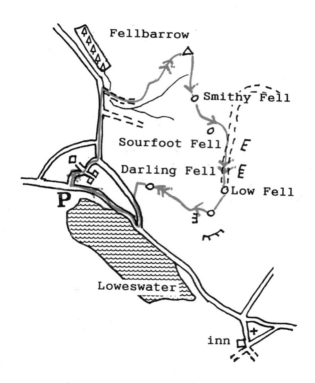

Fellbarrow

Smithy Fell

Sourfoot Fell   E

Darling Fell   E

Low Fell

P

Loweswater

inn

Walk 85

85. Fellbarrow

Ordnance Survey map no: 89/OL 4
Starting point: NY 118224
Walking distance: 8km/5ml
Amount of climbing: 500m/1,660ft

A lovely range of low hills on the fringe on the National Park with quite outstanding views.

Park near the telephone box on the S side of the minor road at the NW end of Loweswater.

Cross the road and follow a sp BRIDLEWAY MOSSERGATE. At a junction turn left and immediately right. Turn left on the lane, pass one track on the right and just over the brow of the hill by some trees double back through a gate on the right. Cross a beck, follow the tractor marks as far as possible, and then follow sheep-tracks through the bracken to pathless, grassy slopes. A fence appearing on the left leads to the TP on Fellbarrow. Turn right and follow the fence. After a short stretch of wall the path swings left to join a green track. Go through a gate and over several stiles to Low Fell and the viewpoint beyond.

Follow the line of the last fence down and then up to Darling Fell. Cross a stile near the summit and follow the ridge down to a fence corner. Keep the fence on your right, cutting the corner when it turns left. A path develops through the bracken down to a stile on the lane. Turn left and on the road turn right for the carpark, using the lakeside path where possible.

Walk 86   Above Holme Wood

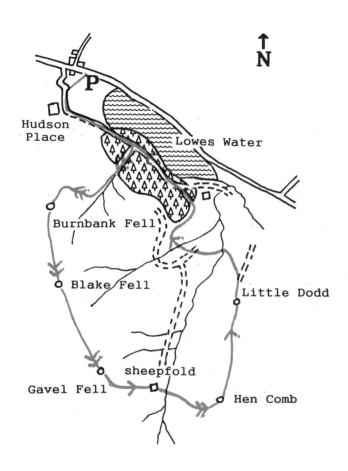

N

P

Hudson
Place

Lowes Water

Burnbank Fell

Blake Fell

Little Dodd

sheepfold

Gavel Fell

Hen Comb

Walk 86

86.   Hen Comb

Ordnance Survey map no: 89/OL 4
Starting point: NY 118224
Walking distance: 13km/8ml
Amount of climbing: 830m/2,700ft

Other people must walk in this area but I have yet to meet
any. Although navigation is made easy in places by a fence,
the route is mostly trackless and some judgment is needed.
    Park as for Walk 85.
    Turn left over a stile a few metres W of the telephone box
and follow a sp to a farm road. Turn left and follow a sp past
the farmhouse on to an enclosed lane. Three hundred metres
after entering the wood, turn right on a broad track leading
up to Holme Force. Climb a small path by the side of the falls.
The path is less used above some stone steps but continues to
a fence. Cross when a section without barbed wire permits
and continue to a crumbling wall at the edge of the wood.
Follow the beck up. Above some sheepfolds climb to the
right on trackless grass. Once on the broad ridge turn left on
a thin path to the fence on the summit of Burnbank Fell, a
surrealistic sculpture of wood, iron and stone.
    Follow the fence S to reach the substantial shelter on Blake
Fell. Continue by the fence and cross a stile on the left at a
fence junction. The fence leads to the cairn on Gavel Fell.
Follow the fence to a bend 300m away, cross the fence, skirt
to right of pools ahead and follow the broad ridge on a
bearing of 110 degrees to a sheepfold in the valley. Cross a
beck, marsh and fence to reach the slopes of Hen Comb and
ascend. Descend on the broad N ridge and cross a minor
summit (Little Dodd). On more level ground do not follow
the track which develops but keep veering left to reach a wall
which crosses the beck. Follow the wall on the opposite side
on a good path through bracken. Cross a track and follow the
wall over a beck and round in a complete U-bend to a gate by
the corner of a wood. A path leads down to the lakeside and
the outward route.
    To shorten the walk, omit the ascent of Hen Comb. Turn
left at the sheepfold and soon find a broad track joining the
main route. Save 0.8km/0.5ml and 250m/825ft of ascent.

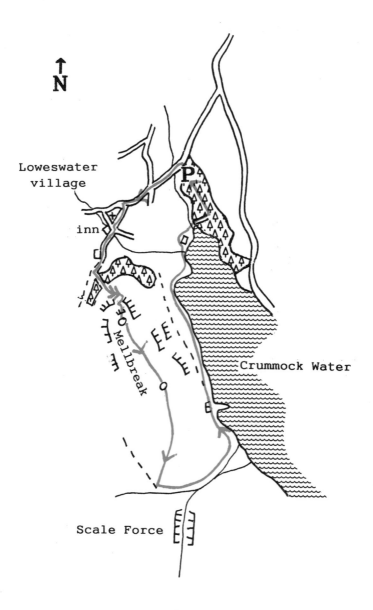

N

Loweswater village

inn

Mellbreak

30

P

Crummock Water

Scale Force

Walk 87

87. *Mellbreak*

Ordnance Survey map no: 89/OL 4
Starting point: NY 149214
Walking distance: 11km/7ml
Amount of climbing: 480m/1,580ft

Mellbreak is an isolated fell gaining attraction from its position above Crummock Water. The short but hard ascent is worth the effort.

The carpark is on the S side of a minor road about 1.5km/1ml E of Loweswater village.

Turn left out of the carpark, cross the bridge, go over the crossroads and turn left down a lane by a telephone box. Pass the church and at the Kirkstile Inn turn left and immediately right at a bridleway sp. Past the farm a stony track leads to a gate, beyond which keep straight ahead between the trees to the open fell. A grassy path leads up to the bottom of a patch of scree. Keep on the path going left until you meet rocks and then turn right again. After some direct ascent take another path left which will lead on to the crest of the ridge above a rock gateway. From here the path is well defined up the ridge to the S top. Keep going N, descending to a broad saddle before climbing to the N top.

Follow the line of some old fence posts until you can see on the fellside opposite the ravine of Scale Force. Aim for it until a path develops which you will see clearly below you through the bracken. You will reach a fence and will probably have to turn right to find a stile and gate at its junction with another fence. Cross the stile and follow the fence down, turning left on a crossing path. This leads to the lakeside where you turn left on a path through often boggy ground. Stay by the lake at the far end of which is the first in a series of stiles leading past a small pumping station to the two bridges of the main outlet. Turn left on a broad, stony track by a bench, ignoring forks to the right, and you will soon be back at the carpark.

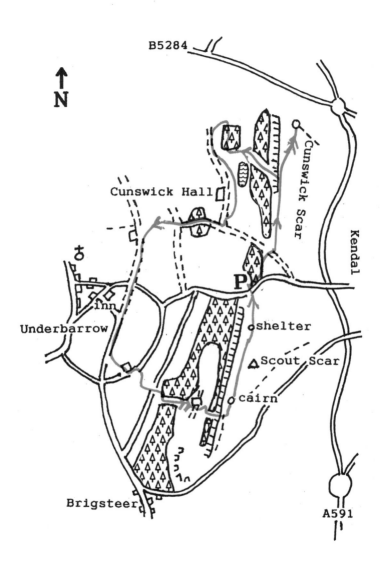

B5284

N

Cunswick Hall

Cunswick Scar

Kendal

P

shelter

Scout Scar

cairn

Inn

Underbarrow

Brigsteer

A591

Walk 88

THE OUTLYING FELLS

88. Cunswick Scar and Scout Scar

Ordnance Survey map no: 97/OL 7
Starting point: SD 488924
Walking distance: 13km/8ml
Amount of climbing: 200m/650ft

An attractive walk over limestone which can give
outstanding views of the Lakeland fells. Only the area
between the carpark and the shelter on Scout Crag is heavily
frequented.

Park in Scout Scar carpark W of Kendal. In Kendal High
Street (one-way traffic) keep in the left lane. Turn left at the
traffic lights opposite the town hall up Allhallows Lane.
Scout Scar is signposted. The carpark is on the right after an
open area by a police transmitter.

Turn left from the carpark on a small path through a wood
parallel to the road. Turn left at a junction with a track to pass
the transmitter and go through the wood to a kissing gate at
the wall corner. Follow the sp PERMISSIVE PATH CUNSWICK
FELL by following a wall on your left and turn left with it to
go N. The wall is succeeded by a fence. Note a kissing gate
which is the point of descent. Take any of the broad tracks
going up to the summit of Cunswick Fell and then return to
the gate and a path through the wood.

Go over a crossing track, cross a stile to the right and leave
the wood by the next gate. Follow a sp to a stile at the left end
of the wood ahead. At the end of the wood turn left to reach
a farm access road. Turn left, go through a gate on the left

191

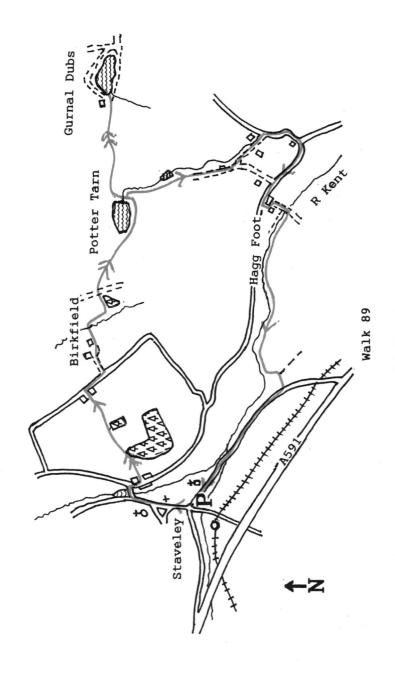

Gurnal Dubs

Potter Tarn

Birkfield

R Kent

Hagg Foot

Staveley

A591

Walk 89

← N

(white arrow), through a second gate and keep to the right-hand edge of the field until a gate gives access back to the track S of Cunswick Hall. At wall junctions turn right and walk with a wall on the left, go through a wood and continue beyond between hedges (very muddy). Cross a farm access road and follow yellow arrows through· gates and stiles downhill, over a track and down to an access road near some cottages. Turn left, cross the lane (inn 250m to the right) and continue between the hedges opposite to reach a lane.

Turn left and left again after 300m on a footpath leading to the drive of a house. Go down the drive, turn left on a lane and after 200m go right at a sp. Cross a bridge and stile, both stone, and go half-right to a gate. Follow a track to a wall junction and turn left to a lane. Turn left and after 20m go up a farm track to the right sp SCOUT SCAR AND KENDAL. Follow the yellow arrows to pass houses on your left and go round the bottom of their gardens and up into a wood. Arrows lead through the wood, across a field and up through a wood again to the right of Barrowfield farm. At the back of the farm go through the left-hand gate and follow a path to the top of the scar. Turn left and follow the tracks on top of the scar past a shelter to the lane and carpark.

To shorten this walk turn left at a sp GAMBLESMIRE LANE where the wall turns N 600m from the carpark. This leads to the track S of Cunswick Hall. Save 3.5km/2ml.

89. *Potter Fell*

Ordnance Survey map no: 97/OL 7
Starting point: SD 470983
Walking distance: 11.5km/7ml
Amount of climbing: 315m/1,040ft

A short, varied walk in an attactive area. You will want to return and explore.

Park in a small carpark on the S side of the main road through Staveley, 50m E of the public toilets.

Turn left out of the carpark and cross the road. Go N along the road sp to Kentmere. Turn right to cross a bridge and fork right at the far side. After 20m turn left between some houses and go through a gate at the end of the cul-de-sac. The route

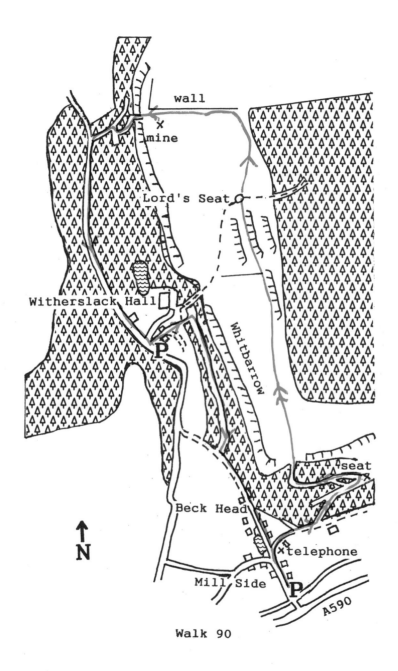

wall

× mine

Lord's Seat ○

Witherslack Hall

P

Whitbarrow

seat

Beck Head

× telephone

Mill Side

P

A590

N

Walk 90

is steeply uphill, following a wall on your left over a series of gates and stiles. Drop downhill to a farm and on to a lane. Turn right and then left to Birkfield. Turn half-right across the farmyard. The path, waymarked on the gate, passes in front of the house before turning sharp right and following a beck on your right. Leave the beck, pass a wood on your right and cross the track beyond a gate. Go half-right uphill on a faint, green path. Through the second gateway in a stone wall on the right follow a bearing of 110 degrees to Potter Tarn. Cross a ladder-stile. Cross the outlet from the tarn and at the far end of the dam cross the wall on the right and go NW to Gurnal Dubs. A path to the left makes a circuit of the tarn, although there is no right of way.

Return to Potter Tarn, cross the outlet and turn left with the beck on your left. Go through a gate and past a small reservoir on your left. Continue downhill to a lane. Turn right and then right again at a T-junction. After 1km turn left at a sp by Hagg Foot farm. Go between the buildings and turn right to the river. Cross and turn right. Follow the riverbank, using stiles and gates as a guide. At the end of a short section between walls go through a kissing gate on the left sp DALES WAY and follow a wall on your right to the next sp. Turn right and right again at the road.

To shorten the walk, omit the section to Gurnal Dubs. Save 1.6km/1ml. A short cut can be taken on the descent from Potter Tarn. Just past a concrete shed on the left the path turns sharp left. Go through a gate on the right on to a bridleway. Pass a farm and turn right at the lane to reach Hagg Foot. Save 1.1km/0.7ml.

90. Whitbarrow

Ordnance Survey map no: 97
Starting point: SD 451840 or SD 437859
Walking distance: 10.5km/6.5ml
Amount of climbing: 205m/680ft

A short walk over a beautiful limestone hill and through lovely woodland in a nature reserve.

To park, turn off the A590 to Barrow into Mill Side village. There is roadside parking on the right after 200m. If this is

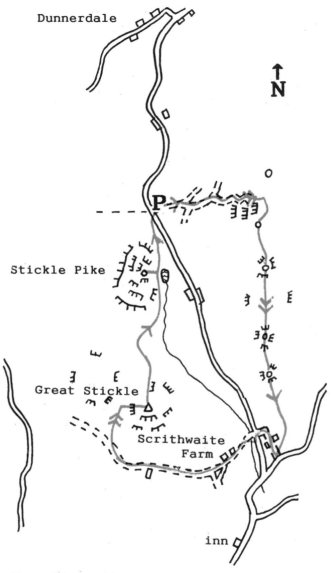

Dunnerdale

N

P

Stickle Pike

Great Stickle

Scrithwaite
Farm

inn

Broughton Mills

Walk 91

full, drive to Witherslack Hall and turn right into a lane by the entrance where there is further parking space and start the walk from this point.

Walk NW towards the village, fork right by a telephone box and immediately right again on a bridleway. Turn right at a junction of tracks and after 200m go left on a track slanting uphill. At a track junction turn right. Turn sharply left just before a seat. The path goes through a gap in the wall on the left and after 20m through a gap on the right. Go NNW for 2.5km over limestone to the summit cairn and memorial. Continue NNW on the main path until a cross wall is met. Turn left, pass the entrance to a drift mine on your left and go through a kissing gate. Descend through woodland by a scree slope. Turn right at a junction by a low post inscribed XI and turn left by a stone wall after 20m. A good track leads to a lane. Turn left, pass a farm on your left and at the foot of the hill turn left on a short lane. Pass some barns and go through a kissing gate. (Alternative parking place. Short walk starts here.) Keep to the left edge of the field, pass a football pitch and cross a stile. Turn right on to a large track through the woods. When this joins a farm track, turn left. Cross a bridge past a spring at the foot of a limestone outcrop and continue to the carpark.

For a shorter walk park by Witherslack Hall and walk as far as the football pitch. Follow a sp on the left to cross the end of the pitch. Further signs and a track lead directly to Lord's Seat where the main route is joined. Save 5.5km/3.5ml.

91. Stickle Pike

Ordnance Survey map no: 96/OL 6
Starting point: SD 214933
Walking distance: 6.5km/4ml
Amount of climbing: 400m/1,300ft

A highly recommended walk over broken, rocky terrain in a quiet corner of Lakeland.

Park at the top of the fell road N of Broughton Mills.

Follow the green path going E and shortly fork right, dropping to a rutted track. Take a path on the right winding

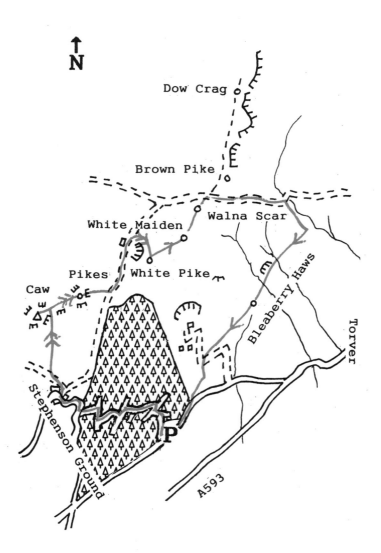

Walk 92

up among the quarries. Once above them turn right on to the ridge above. A narrow path goes along the ridge but omits the high points. It leads through bracken to a gate and stile. Cross neither but double back right on a green path. Go through a gate, turn right, cross a stile and pass between the farm buildings to the lane. Cross the stile opposite, ford the beck and join the track going past the front of Scrithwaite farm. Go through the farm gate ahead and at a picnic table turn right into a walled lane. Pass a barn and gate, 100m beyond which a path rises to the right on to the open fell. At a co! turn right over rough ground to the TP on Great Stickle.

From here Stickle Pike can be seen to the N. A good path gradually develops, skirting a marshy area and rising as a broad grassy track to a col. From the second cairn a worn path leads to the summit. Retrace your steps to the cairn and follow the path down to the carpark.

92. Caw

Ordnance Survey map no: 96/OL 6
Starting point: SD 252927
Walking distance: 14.5km/9ml
Amount of climbing: 730m/2,400ft

An excellent walk which is generally very quiet and has extensive views of the Scafell range.

Park in a Forestry Commission carpark/picnic area on a minor road S of Torver.

Cross the stile at the back of the carpark and follow a path down to a forest road. Turn left and then right at a nearby junction. Double back to the left on a stony track going downhill. Cross a beck and go uphill, ignoring the track to the left by the sheds. Turn left at the next junction and soon turn right by a blue arrow on to a path winding through the forest and a sp by blue paint marks. Turn right at a forest road and take the first turning on the left down to a lane. Here turn right and by the buildings of Stephenson Ground farm go through a gate on the right with a bridleway sp and turn left to pass behind the farm on a path between walls. From the second gate a path goes straight ahead through bracken on the open fell towards Caw, the left-hand of the two peaks

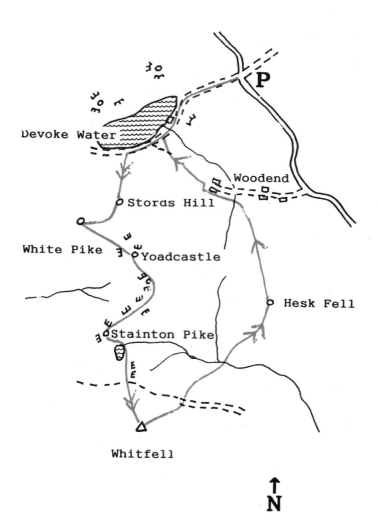

Devoke Water

Woodend

P

Storas Hill

White Pike

Yoadcastle

Hesk Fell

Stainton Pike

Whitfell

↑
N

Walk 93

ahead. When there is no path follow the beck towards Caw. An easy way up the last slopes is to the left from a col.

From the TP go back to the col and continue NE over the nearby summit of Pikes and then down to a col where a broad track is met. Turn left and follow it just past some old quarry buildings. Turn right and climb the grassy slopes to the cairn on White Pike. Make your way to White Maiden to which the wall in front leads and continue on the ridge to Walna Scar and down to the old track over the pass.

Turn right and descend as far as the pack-horse bridge. Do not cross it but turn right on a path parallel to the beck until you have almost reached a sheepfold by a wall. Turn right on a path, which follows this wall at a little distance, as far as a quarry. Go straight through the quarry and cross the beck on to a muddy track which soon becomes a small clear path going over the grassy hill in front. The path descends through a boggy area to a gap in a wall with just a low piece of wire to cross. Continue to the surfaced quarry road on a bend by some posts. Head S towards a green ramp which you can see rising from left to right. Cross a very marshy area at its narrowest point which is at the bottom of this ramp. At the top a rough stile leads to the road. The carpark is 500m to the right.

To shorten the walk follow the wall S from White Maiden to reach the quarry road on the bend as described above. Save 4km/2.5ml.

93. Whit Fell

Ordnance Survey map no: 96/OL 6
Starting point: SD 171977
Walking distance: 14km/9ml
Amount of climbing: 650m/2,150ft

The route is over a series of rocky tors with no paths and has unrivalled views of the peaks around Wasdale and Eskdale. For both reasons, clear weather is essential.

Park E of the minor road between Eskdale Green and Ulpha by the sp to Stanley Gill.

Cross the road and go along the stony track leading SW to Devoke Water. Pass the boathouse and stay on the lakeside path until opposite an island. Turn left up a little ridge to the

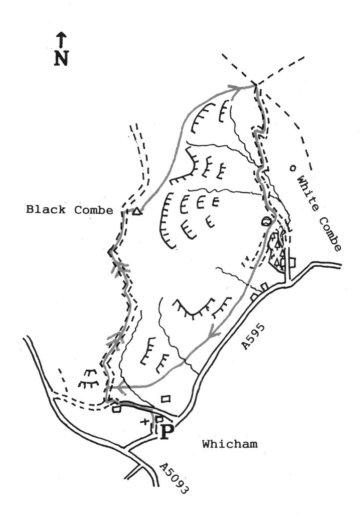

N

Black Combe

o White Combe

A595

Whicham

P

A5093

Walk 94

grassy knoll of Stords Hill. The next objective, White Pike, is
at 220 degrees but to reach it curve to the left first. From its
large cairn follow a bearing of 110 degrees to Yoadcastle, a
cairn on the skyline. Pass to the left of the next tor then curve
around the head of a valley and below the base of a low rocky
tor to reach the little ridge leading to Stainton Pike. Cross a
fence just before reaching the summit. Cross the fence again
to the drier ground on the far side of Holehouse Tarn and keep
to a line of low rocks to reach the base of Whit Fell.

Climb to the summit with a TP, shelter and huge cairn. For
Hesk Fell, the final peak, follow a bearing of 70 degrees
down to a bridleway and wall. The next section is boggy.
Follow the wall to the left to a large gap at a fence junction.
Cross so that the fence is on your left and follow it to a
junction with another fence. Cross the fence on your left and
then the wall and the beck behind it. Follow the wall to
sheepfolds and then turn left to reach the tiny cairn on the
grassy summit. Descend on a bearing of 330 degrees and at
a wall turn left and follow it as far as a gate by a barn. Here
turn left on a muddy path going over a rise, take a right fork
and join the lakeside path. Turn right and pass the boathouse
on the return to the road.

94. Black Combe

Ordnance Survey map no: 96
Starting point: SD 135826
Walking distance: 12km/7.5ml
Amount of climbing: 600m/2,000ft

A fine hill to climb, with well-made, easy paths giving fine
views of the Lancashire coast, Isle of Man and the Galloway
Hills, as well as of the fells.

Park outside Whicham church or in a lay-by off the A595
by the entrance to the short driveway.

Walk between the church and the buildings on its right (an
old school) turn left on a lane and continue on a stony track
past a farm. Turn right on to a green track through a gate.
Follow this well-graded path until a huge stone arrow
pointing to the right indicates the way to the TP and shelter
on the summit.

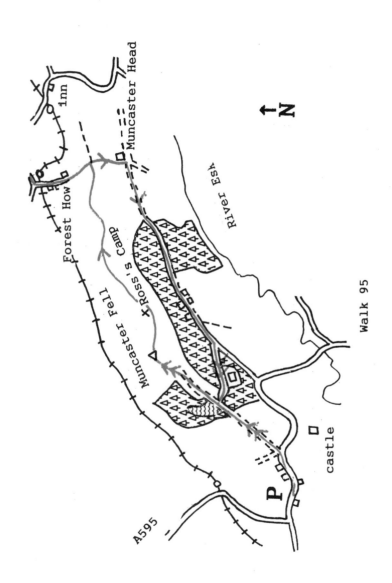

Inn

Muncaster Head

Forest How

River Esk

Ross's Camp

Muncaster Fell

N

Walk 95

castle

P

A595

Follow the edge of the cliffs on your right on a bearing of 40 degrees for 2km and before the ground begins to rise again, go through a boggy patch on to a broad, green path zig-zagging downhill to the right. Cross the beck and fork left. Just before reaching a wall and a wood, turn right immediately below a pond to reach a track by the wall. When the track curves right, leave it and follow the wall/fence on sheep-tracks/paths to the outward route. Turn left for the carpark.

95. *Muncaster Fell*

Ordnance Survery map no: 96/OL 6
Starting point: SD 097967
Walking distance: 14km/8.5ml
Amount of climbing: 300m/1,000ft

This walk makes a full day when combined with a visit to Muncaster Castle. There are good views up Eskdale and a chance to see the narrow-gauge railway.

Park in a large carpark opposite the castle on the N side of the A595.

Turn left from the carpark (no footpath for 50m) and when the road bends right keep straight ahead at a sp PUBLIC BRIDLEWAY MUNCASTER FELL. The TP on the summit is reached by a path from the corner of a plantation, the path continuing and rejoining the track, now grassy, by a boggy patch. Pass a stone table (ROSS'S CAMP 1883) and go through a gateway. The track climbs again on a stone ramp and descends to a gate. Turn left at the next wall at a sp IRTON ROAD, ESKDALE GREEN. Past Forest How the lane leads to the railway (trains on the half hour). Turn right to the village store and toilets. Retrace your steps past Forest How and follow the sp for Muncaster Head. Past the farm turn right on to a stony track and fork right at a sp for Muncaster. Past some cottages the track is surfaced. Turn right at a sp BRIDLEWAY by some old sheds and turn left at a junction with your outward route.

To shorten the walk omit the visit to the railway and village. Save 2.5km/1.5ml.

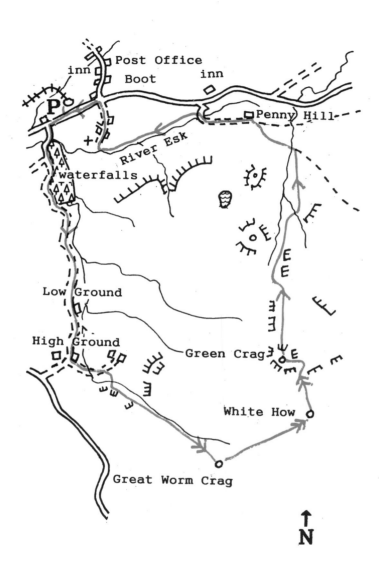

Post Office

inn

Boot

inn

P

Penny Hill

River Esk

waterfalls

Low Ground

High Ground

Green Crag

White How

Great Worm Crag

N

Walk 96

96. Green Crag

Ordnance Survey map no: 89 and 96/OL 6
Starting point: NY 172007
Walking distance: 13.5km/8.5ml
Amount of climbing: 550m/1,800ft

Despite one very boggy stretch this remains a delightful walk which you will find quite solitary, with waterfalls, crags, views of all the highest peaks and a lovely riverside path at the end. Much of the route is pathless and it needs a clear day.

Use the NT carpark by Dalegarth station in Eskdale.

Turn right from the carpark and go left up the first lane, sp to Dalegarth Falls. Take the left fork sp WATERFALLS. (To visit the falls go through a kissing gate on your left and follow any of the routes upstream. Whichever exit you come to on the boundary wall, continue S for 100m to reach the track you left earlier and turn left.) The track passes Low Ground and then goes through the farmyard of High Ground on to a surfaced road. When this bends right fork left on a stony track by a wall. About 200m past a gate the wall turns left. At this point go half-right, aiming for a small crag low on the hillside. In a few moments you will see a stile which you cross. Great Worm Crag is ahead (bearing 140 degrees) but immediately in front is a marshy area. The best way round is to turn right and then left to cross a beck directly in front of the nearer of two rocky outcrops. From here take the best way you can through the bog to another outcrop. Not far beyond this the beck runs freely and the ground is drier. Follow the beck until you reach the firmer ground ahead and climb directly to the summit.

The next objective is the knoll of White How (bearing 70 degrees). From there turn left, now going N, for the slopes of Green Crag and pick your way on grass between the rocks to the summit. A clear path leads N to a col (there is a parish boundary stone to your left) and rises again. It now continues along a shelf on the ridge with the main crags above you on your left. It then descends to another col and continues, the high ground now on the right. The path becomes intermittent but is occasionally cairned and is making for the right-hand side of the valley, following the line of a beck on your left.

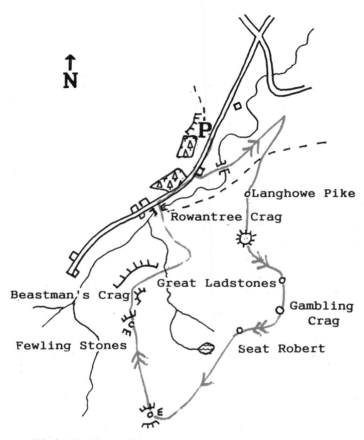

N

oLanghowe Pike

Rowantree Crag

Great Ladstones

Beastman's Crag

Gambling
Crag

Fewling Stones

Seat Robert

High Wether Howe

Walk 97

When you meet a construction of angle iron, cross the small beck and turn left to continue downhill as before. A cairned and larger path develops. Take a fork to the left to cross the beck that you have been following.

You now follow a sp path with a wall on your right leading down through Penny Hill farm to Doctor Bridge. Cross, turn left and follow the river to St Margaret's church from where a lane leads to the road. Turn left for the carpark.

97. Seat Robert

Ordnance Survey Map No: 90/OL 5
Starting point: NY 521141
Walking distance: 10.5km/6.5ml
Amount of climbing: 335ml/1,110ft

As most of this walk is over trackless ground, progress is slower than might be anticipated. Views take in the Pennines and Howgills and the solitude is something to be savoured.

Park in a large, grassy parking area on the N side of a minor road 500m beyond the waterworks filter-house. Reach it by following the sp to Haweswater from Shap, then the sp to Rosthwaite. Take a sharp turning left at the sp to Swindale and go straight over at the crossroads.

Go S on the lane and turn left at a sp by Swindale Foot farm. The path continues beyond the farmyard gate and forks left to reach a footbridge. Keep the next wall on your right and go through a gate. The path fades in a boggy patch but rises to the right through bracken shortly past the first telegraph pole. Aim for a solitary telephone pole on the skyline and having reached it, turn right uphill to a wall. Turn right and when the wall curves left, leave it, cross a track and climb the low rocks ahead. Go S for the little cairn on Langhowe Pike 500m away. Continue 600m to the S to Rowantree Crag, a dark upthrust of rock with a holly tree on the S side. The next objective, Great Ladstones, is another 600m on a bearing of 150 degrees, its cairn visible on the skyline. From here go S to Gambling Crag (no cairn) and then continue S to a wall. Turn right and at the top of the rise go up right to reach the cairn, shelter and Ordnance Survey ring on Seat Robert.

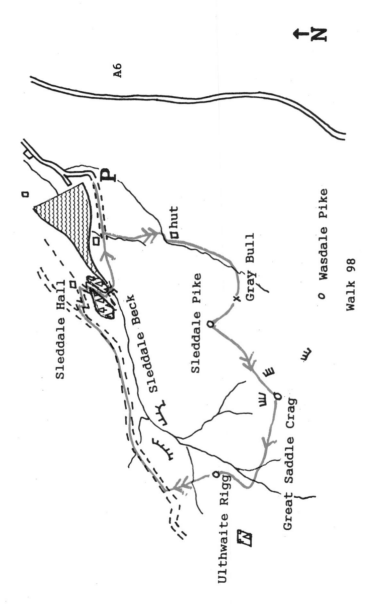

N

A6

P

□ hut

Sleddale Hall

Sleddale Beck

Sleddale Pike

Gray Bull

x

Great Saddle Crag

Ulthwaite Rigg

o Wasdale Pike

Walk 98

Go SW and join a fence which passes the S foot of High Wether Howe. From the summit go N on the highest ground over rock outcrops until a wall is seen ahead from the last (Fewling Stones). Go to the left of the isolated outcrop of Beastman's Crag and turn right, picking up a good track. When the wall on your left turns left, keep straight ahead through marshy ground until the wall reappears on your left. Cross the beck, make for a large cairn on the slope opposite and turn left on a grassy track which becomes more definite and leads down through bracken to a footbridge and lane. Turn right for the carpark.

98.   *Wet Sleddale*

Ordnance Survey map no: 90/OL 5 and 7
Starting point: NY 555114
Walking distance: 13km/8ml
Amount of climbing: 410m/1,350ft

Most of this walk is trackless, offering, on a fine day, a good opportunity to test your map-reading skills. Although it is not like the main Lakeland fells, this is still splendid walking country with deer and buzzards among other attractions.

Park in the carpark at the end of Wet Sleddale reservoir reached by a minor road sp 20m S of the A6/M6 link from Junction 38.

Follow the bridleway sp from the end of the carpark and fork right, keeping by the reservoir as far as New Ing barn among the trees. Turn left uphill with a wall on your right. Shortly after passing through a gate, follow the beck. A line of corrugated-iron shooting butts leads to a bridge and shooting hut to the right. Continue on rough vehicle-tracks until past the last of the butts, then cross the beck on your right to reach Gray Bull, a large boulder prominent on the skyline. Go across trackless heather on a bearing of 290 degrees to the cairn visible on Sleddale Pike.

Take a bearing of 220 degrees to the cairn on Great Saddle Crag. Cross a fence and go over grassy slopes between crags to the summit. The next objective, Ulthwaite Rigg, is the end of the second ridge to the NW. To reach it, follow a bearing of 270 degrees initially, aiming for the right edge of a small

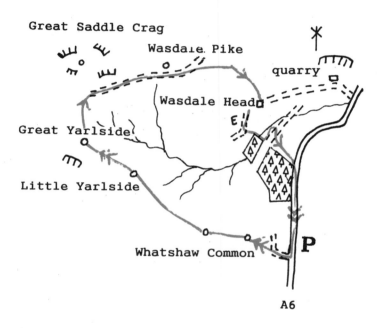

Great Saddle Crag

Wasdale Pike

quarry

Wasdale Head

Great Yarlside

Little Yarlside

Whatshaw Common

N

P

A6

Walk 99

plantation in the distance while negotiating heather and bogs by sheep-tracks. After crossing Sleddale Beck curve right for the uncairned summit. Continue on a bearing of 60 degrees to reach a bridleway beyond an area of drainage ditches. Turn right. Fifty metres after passing through the second gate fork right on a zig-zag track down to the abandoned Sleddale Hall. Keep on the main zig-zag track sp with white arrows through a wood. Cross a stile on your left to a reproduction pack-horse bridge and follow white-topped posts to the left beyond a gate. The posts lead across boggy ground, through a gap in a wall, over a beck and through a gate to New Ings and your outward route.

99. Wasdale Horseshoe

Ordnance Survey map no: 90/OL 7
Starting point: NY 554062
Walking distance: 9.5km/6ml
Amount of climbing: 350m/1,150ft

This is the other Wasdale that used to be in Westmorland when it existed. Just inside the National Park, it offers, like other walks in the area, a peaceful environment for recreation.

Park near a telephone box in a large lay-by on the summit of the A6, either side of road.

About 80m S of the telephone box go through a gate on the W side of the road on to a grassy track. When this turns right keep ahead with the wall/fence on your left. Beyond Whatshaw Common at a junction of fences follow the fence to the right, crossing over for a few metres to avoid a bog and crossing back by a wall. Follow this wall down into Wasdale Mouth and up over Great Yarlside. The summit and a sunken Ordnance Survey ring are just over the wall. At the wall end cross a section of wooden fencing and turn right, following the fence E, and pick up a vehicle-track. This leads to within 20m of the summit of Wasdale Pike and close to a rain-gauge on your right. A hundred metres beyond the summit the track curves left. At this point branch right on a sheep-track on a bearing of 120 degrees. When the track dies out maintain direction, aiming for the TV mast on the hill ahead until a

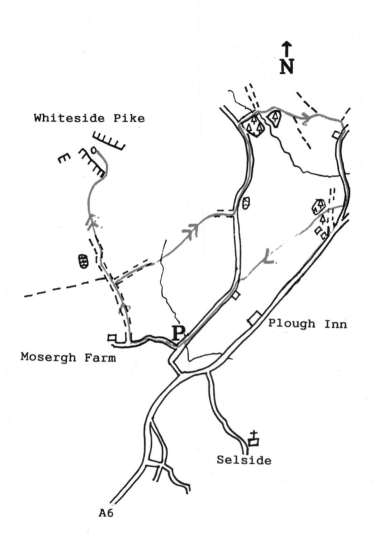

Whiteside Pike

N

Plough Inn

Mosergh Farm

P

Selside

A6

Walk 100

ruined farm is sighted in the valley. Cross a fence and follow the next fence down to a junction with a wall. Turn left and cross a blocked gate for access to the ruins. Turn right on a track and when it begins to climb and turns right, leave it and continue by a wall, turning left through a gate. Follow the plantation on your right and then aim half-left for a gate in a fence across the hillside. Continue uphill by the plantation to a wired-up gate on the road. Turn right for the carpark.

100. Whiteside Pike

Ordnance Survey map no: 90 and 97/OL 7
Starting point: NY 530999
Walking distance: 9.5km/6ml
Amount of climbing: 250m/825ft

A walk of great charm especially in early summer, to a peak with more distinction than its Buttermere near namesake.

Parking is near the Plough Inn, 8km/5ml N of Kendal on the A6. Turn W 500m S of the inn on a lane sp to Mosergh farm. Pass a turning on the left and park on the wide verge near a small bridge.

Walk back towards the main road and turn right at the sp to Mosergh farm. Fork right before the farm at a bridleway sp. Note a lane between walls on the right and pass a bridleway sp on the left. Continue to the end of the enclosed track and on to the open fell. The rough track peters out but a route can be picked out by sheep-tracks to a cairn on the rocky summit which is clearly visible ahead. Return by your outward route as far as the walled lane passed earlier and turn left. Go through a gate and continue uphill with a wall on your right before turning to the right between walls and reaching a lane. (To shorten the walk turn right. Save 4km/2.5ml.)

Turn left and follow the lane to the far end of a plantation in the valley. Turn right, go over a bridge and through a gate. Turn right immediately and a path becomes more definite as you approach a wall. The path becomes vague again at the top of the rise but it curves left and makes for a gate in the fence ahead. Cross a small beck 50m beyond and take the left fork going up the rise in front. Maintain direction until the

Walk 100   On the A6

path becomes more pronounced as it curves to the right across the hillside. Follow a wall and at a junction with another wall go through a farm gate on your right (not through a small gate in front). This leads down to a lane where you turn right. Just before the A6 go through a gate on the right sp as a bridleway and continue by the wall to a driveway which you cross, rising slightly to a small plantation. You are now on the embankment of an old road, locally called the Roman Road, which leads through gates to a lane. Turn left for the carpark.

AUTHOR'S COMMENTS
AND HINTS

Getting to the Start

It is no longer possible to reach the start of more than a handful of the routes in this book by public transport but if you are staying in the Lake District a short drive from a suitable centre is all that is needed. Wherever possible, the parking area suggested is an official carpark provided by town or village authorities or the National Trust or the National Park. Many of these are Pay and Display, but for your money there are frequently toilets, refreshments and information points. Where this is not the case, please take care not to obstruct side-roads or gates into fields, and for your own benefit watch for ditches hidden by long grass and do not park on soft ground. If there is a house or farm nearby it would be in your interest to let the occupants know that you are leaving the car intentionally.

Many country carparks now warn against theft from vehicles. Leave nothing on view and take all valuables with you.

Clothing

There is scope for individual choice of clothing for hill walking but you must be prepared for much wider swings in temperature and other conditions than are met off the hills. A combination of wind, cold and rain can be life-threatening and you must be prepared to meet this.

Footwear – in fine weather a few of the low-altitude walks in this book can be done in good-quality trainers, although personally I prefer to wear lightweight fabric boots. The only real choice for mountains is leather boots with full bellows tongue and a strong sole with good tread. Over-waxing can rot them but they will need occasional treatment. Wet boots should be dried away from direct heat and with crumpled newspaper inside.

Outer-wear – the wind- and waterproof anorak that is needed will also build up excessive heat and condensation inside and solutions of this problem can be extremely expensive. I would advise against buying the cheapest on the market; watch for sales of last year's models and colours – the market is now very fashion-conscious. On most models the zip fastening is covered with a flap closed by velcro. A hood is essential.

Mid-wear – shirt and woollen sweater are still used by many but the fleece jackets now available have many advantages. Again, if you don't mind last season's colours you'll find a better buy.

Underwear – whatever your prejudices, you will appreciate a set of thermals in winter.

Leg-wear – I find breeches convenient but they have never been regarded as essential as they are on the continent. Old trousers or track-suit bottoms are adequate in summer provided that you also have over-trousers (see comments on anoraks). Gaiters are useful.

Hat and gloves – you will need to carry both even if you don't use them all the time. In the cold carry a woollen or fleece hat; in summer take a sunhat if you suffer from heat. Woollen gloves and also waterproof mitts are useful.

Socks – all walkers used to wear two pairs of socks but modern boots are usually well padded and one pair of loop-pile socks is enough for most people.

Spare clothing – sweaters, scarf, etc. according to season.

Equipment

Rucksack – a wide choice is available but, again, bottom-of-the-market models are not durable. For day walks, 25 to 35 litres capacity is about right. Look for a model with two side pockets, a padded back and curved straps. Fit a cord grip if there isn't one and don't assume that the sac will be waterproof – use a plastic bin liner or something stronger inside.

Map – always have the recommended map with you and carry it in a map case or a freezer bag in bad weather. The legend on the map explains all about compass bearings, grid references and scales.

Compass – buy one of the Silva type with bearings in degrees. It is outside the scope of this book to give instruction in its use but all hill walkers will have to learn. The Ramblers' Association has recently published a standardised course on navigation which will soon be widely available through its groups and there are many books on the market.

Whistle – buy a non-metallic one that will not interfere with the workings of your compass. The international distress signal is six blasts at regular intervals repeated at intervals of one minute.

Torch – I always carry a small one whatever the season, but in winter a larger one is essential. As a distress signal, the pattern is the same as with a whistle. (Camera flash has been used successfully.)

First Aid – plasters, wound dressings and pain-killers are all that most people take. A group should consider taking more: several triangular bandages, insect repellent and Waspeze, antiseptic wipes, elastic bandages and knee/ankle supports.

Food and drink – according to taste! It is better to carry more food than you are likely to need as you will use a lot of energy during the day. At all events, it is essential that emergency food is carried over and above what you plan to eat during the walk. This is best in the form of chocolate, Kendal Mint Cake, etc. and will need replacing at intervals.

Other items – the list is endless, but you could consider: binoculars, a square of closed-cell foam to sit on, a walking staff (particularly one of the new lightweight telescopic ones), a Swiss army knife, a pedometer, a short length of towelling to use as scarf or towel, or to lay over barbed wire, an ice axe in winter, a plastic bivouac bag for emergencies.

On the Walk

Just how the day goes will depend on a number of factors. If you are on your own then you will not be bothered by somebody else's fast or slow pace. You will, however, be limited to safer ground, better weather and more familiar areas for safety's sake. Three or four in a group provides a margin of safety in emergencies but large groups, while they have their merits, are inevitably slower. If it takes one person 30 seconds to cross a stile and there are 23 stiles and 30 in the group, then it is not difficult to see how a large group will extend the time taken. Similarly, all the breaks seem to extend themselves and the leader has to plan for this.

A reasonable estimate of walking time for an adult may be made by allowing 12 minutes per kilometre plus an additional minute for each ten metres of altitude to be gained (or 20 minutes per mile and three minutes for every 100 feet). Also allow a ten-minute rest for each hour of walking. Other factors may affect your speed: errors of navigation, head winds, rough terrain, minor emergencies. Allow for all this when planning the walk and enjoy the extra time in the pub if you don't need it.

Always make a final check of your equipment before setting off and, having done so, avoid the common mistake of rushing off at a fast pace. I have seen people do this even on the first day of the Pennine Way. By walking steadily the body will warm up before the big efforts are needed and have something in reserve at the end of a long day or if an emergency arises. Keep up a steady pace without too many short stops. When you do stop, look for somewhere out of the wind and put some reserve clothing on. Mountain tops are not usually the best place for lunch but generally somewhere sheltered can be found not too far off. Keep the party together whatever the conditions and however close the carpark. Accidents, small or big, tend to happen when you are tired, and a rush for the car is as likely a cause as any. In mist it is essential that you all keep close.

If I have made hill walking sound very daunting it is because I wish to stress that in bad weather and in winter conditions mountains are essentially a hostile environment, particularly for the urban creatures that most of us are. Planning, the right equipment, the right companions, fitness and experience will all help you to a state where the dangers are controlled and you can enjoy the many physical and aesthetic delights of the hills.

If you are in trouble then try self-help first. In bad weather lose height quickly but safely – you are rarely far from a road and a telephone in the Lake District. If one of your party cannot get off the fells then, after having done what you can to make that person safe and comfortable, make a note of the position of the casualty and of other details, such as time of the incident, nature of injuries, number in the party still on the fell, and make your way to a telephone. Ring 999 and ask for the police. They will call out the mountain-rescue team. Don't sit around and assume that somebody will come looking for you, particularly if you have left no note of your intended route. To have done this is a wise precaution.

The Weather

I have already made much of this as it is such an important factor both for safety and enjoyment. If you take the advice given above, you will have prepared for the worst. All you can do is check the weather forecasts and hope for the best. Air temperature falls by about 4°F per 1,000ft, whatever the weather, which is something to bear in mind when listening to weather forecasts. On the other hand, when the valleys are full of mist the sun can shine with brilliance on the mountain tops.

If you go out walking on a regular basis, don't be put off by the weather. It can often turn out much better than it is early in the day. Apart from that, if properly protected, walking in any weather can be enjoyable.

An accurate, local forecast is available round the clock by phoning 05394 45151.

Rights and Responsibilities

There has always been some conflict of interest between those who make their living from the land and those who use the countryside for enjoyment. At times I have been incensed by blocked footpaths, misleading or aggressive notices, by dogs, bulls and angry people. But not often. Farmers have a lot to put up with from some of the visitors they encounter and a considerate walker may get the backlash sometimes. I have met more helpful farmers than otherwise and have been grateful more than once for the initative their wives show in selling tea and home-made cake. Many footpaths to the hills pass through a farmyard and rather than walk by in embarrassed silence try passing the time of day – usually you will meet with success.

The Country Code was devised to try to ease some of these tensions and it is worth repeating it here:

Enjoy the countryside and respect its life and work
Guard against all risk of fire
Fasten all gates
Keep your dogs under close control
Keep to rights of way across farmland
Use stiles and gates to cross fences, hedges and walls
Leave livestock, crops and machinery alone
Take your litter home
Help to keep all water clean
Protect wildlife, plants and trees
Take special care on country roads
Make no unnecessary noise.

To the best of the author's knowledge the walks in this book are on rights of way or in areas where there are access agreements or on established routes that are not subject to dispute.

In my view the walker's best defence against encroachments of the right to walk in the countryside is to join the Ramblers' Association whose address is:

1/5 Wandsworth Road
London SW8 2XX
Tel: 071 582 6878

In addition, I would recommend joining the National Trust to support their work in the Lake District. It gives the added advantage of the free use of their many carparks so that keen walkers will soon get their money back. Their address is:

The National Trust Membership Department
PO Box 39
Bromley
Kent BR1 1NH

INDEX OF PLACES